T0193314

Sartre and Clio

Sartre and Clio

Encounters with History

Mark Hulliung

Routledge
Taylor & Francis Group

LONDON AND NEW YORK

First published 2014 by Paradigm Publishers

Published 2016 by Routledge
2 Park Square, Milton Park, Abingdon, Oxon OX14 4RN
711 Third Avenue, New York, NY 10017, USA

Routledge is an imprint of the Taylor & Francis Group, an informa business

Copyright © 2014, Taylor & Francis.

Library of Congress Cataloging-in-Publication Data
Hulliung, Mark.
 Sartre and Clio : encounters with history / Mark Hulliung.
   p. cm.
 Includes bibliographical references and index.
 ISBN 978-1-61205-044-7 (hardcover : alk. paper)
 ISBN 978-1-61205-045-4 (paperback : alk. paper)
1. Sartre, Jean-Paul, 1905–1980—Political and social views. I. Title.
 JC261.S372H85 2012
 901—dc23

2012019309

Designed and Typeset by Straight Creek Bookmakers.

ISBN 13 : 978-1-61205-044-7 (hbk)
ISBN 13 : 978-1-61205-045-4 (pbk)

*To Barbara and Peter
the best of friends*

Contents

Preface and Acknowledgments

The purpose of this book is to offer a study of the changing role of history in the thought of Jean-Paul Sartre, from *Nausea* in 1938 to his final writings, with a number of fascinating complications along the way.

My study covers not all but a great many of Sartre's writings, as dictated by the theme. It is written in a style that is open to the larger public, not simply the experts. The modest length of my study, the importance of its central concern, and its jargon-free prose will, I hope, invite the maximum number of readers.

Throughout this volume, I have used the standard translations of Sartre's works whenever they exist, but I have not hesitated to provide my own revised versions when necessary. When citing a text that has never appeared in English, the translations are my own.

My debts are to the scholars who have preceded me and to the students who have repeatedly reminded me that Sartre still matters.

Chapter 1

To Historicize or Not to Historicize

The vogue of Jean-Paul Sartre may not be what it once was, but as anyone who teaches undergraduates knows, there is no lack of young people who remain enthusiastic about grappling with his writings. A coterie of scholars, too, seems determined to prove that rumors of Sartre's intellectual death and irrelevance are greatly exaggerated. Partly this continuing scholarly output is a matter of the successful recovery in recent years of what his biographer Annie Cohen-Solal spoke of in 1985 as the "thousands of his pages scattered around the world."[1] Even more, his refusal to disappear is attributable to the reality that, love him or hate him, one cannot deny him admittance to the ranks of the great minds of his century. Sartre remains a figure of keen interest.

Is there anything new to say about Sartre? There is and will continue to be because new perspectives can always be brought to bear upon familiar materials. What I shall attempt is a study of the changing role of history in his thought, from *Nausea* in 1938 to his final major efforts, the two-volume *Critique of Dialectical Reason* and the multivolume study of Flaubert, *Idiot of the Family,* with many unexpected, perplexing, and fascinating stops, reversals, and zigzags along the way. While many secondary works on Sartre touch on my topic, their focus is elsewhere. Despite the wealth of the secondary literature, I believe there is something to be said about Sartre that is new and significant.

In *Nausea,* the book that made him famous, Sartre denounced the writing of history as a doubly worthless pursuit, first because it is untruthful and second because it is useless except as an attempt to escape from our very selves. But by the time he published the first volume of the *Critique of Dialectical Reason,* he dared announce his extraordinary ambition that the second tome "will attempt to establish that there is *one* human history, with *one* truth and *one* intelligibility."[2] He also declared that to write history and to be engaged politically were intimately interrelated activities, a fusion of theory and practice. Sartre began by repudiating Clio and ended by embracing her, eventually asking far more of the study of history, it seems, than any other thinker of his age or more recent times.

It would be a mistake, however, to conclude that a line of development runs straight and true from *Nausea* in 1938 to the *Critique* in 1960. Sartre's encounter with Clio was an on-again, off-again affair, a stormy relationship with many break-ups and an unsatisfying finale. Only posthumously, in 1985, was the long-awaited sequel to volume one of the *Critique of Dialectical Reason* released, and then in a frustratingly truncated, imperfectly organized form. Of the *Critique,* it may be argued that of all his unfinished projects this was one he simply had to bring to fruition, that his life's work was seriously incomplete in its absence. Why two decades after publication of the first volume was the second *Critique* unfinished and misshapen? How did it happen that a book he had already sketched in 1958, two years before the appearance of volume one, and that he announced in 1959 would be released "within a year,"[3] remained incomplete in 1980, the year of his death?

If failure to finish the *Critique* is one measure of Sartre's difficulties in coming to terms with historical reason, another is his long record of advancing the study of history in some publications while simultaneously seeking to write history out of his work in others. On the one hand, there is the Sartre who, after elaborating his method of "existential psychoanalysis" in *Being and Nothingness* (1943), called upon it when he decided to write history in the form of biographies of Baudelaire and Jean Genet, an interest that began during World War II and that he carried with him to his dying day, still working at the end of his life on the finale to his massive biographical study of Flaubert (below, Chapter 2, "From Time to History").

On the other hand is a contrasting Sartre who is likewise a product of the immediate postwar era and a forceful presence in his thought for many years thereafter. Quite striking is this second Sartre's protracted fascination with groups that, he believed, have been denied a history: the French during the German occupation, Jews throughout the centuries, the French proletarians of the early 1950s, pre-1959 Cubans, and the victims of Western colonialism in Algeria and elsewhere (below, Chapter 3, "The Historical Search for the Unhistorical"). The reason he was so fascinated with these victims, caught in repetition and denied a past, is perhaps not impossible to discern. Very likely it was because he believed that if anyone was likely to heed the call to "authenticity" it was these groups, facing hopeless or seemingly hopeless odds, yet fortunately denied by their misfortunes the temptation of members of other groups to lose themselves in the past. Unlike the rest of us, members of these groups, standing outside history, were forced to face up to the choice between authentic and inauthentic existence.

In the fourth chapter ("Human History and the Human Condition"), we shall discuss yet another reason why Sartre was sometimes reluctant to follow the path to history and all-out historicity. Along with Albert Camus, Sartre vehemently rejected "humanism" in his earlier writings, only to reinstate it in revised form as World War II drew to a close. Soon, this revisiting of humanism included a reworking of the notion of "the human condition," which figures prominently in the French intellectual tradition from Montaigne and Pascal to Malraux and beyond. Although there is no human essence or human nature, there is a fixed, static, unchanging human condition in which time may matter, as in Beckett and Sartre, but history does not. A tension in Sartre's thought arguably exists between his attraction to the notion of the human condition and his desire to solve the problem of history. That tension was fated to be greatly aggravated when Camus called on his understanding of "the human condition" to repudiate the French Communist party, the Soviet Union, and their historicist philosophies at exactly the same time that Sartre was entering his most intense period of "fellow-traveling."

Chapter 5, "History and Revolution," marks a new emphasis. In the writings of Sartre that we shall examine in Chapters 3 and 4, he frequently speaks to us in the language of "resistance" and "refusal": the French who resisted the Nazis, the Jews who resist the anti-Semites, and so forth. But in Chapter 5, where the *Critique* is one of the foremost primary sources, he consistently speaks the language not of resistance but of "revolution."

The Sartre who placed history at the top of his agenda in the *Critique* shared something fundamental with the earlier Sartre who cared little for historical studies: In both cases, his concern was that we should not turn to history to escape into the past. Previously drawn to groups denied a past, he was preoccupied in the *Critique* with groups that forge a revolutionary new future rather than accept a continuation of the past. The old word "authenticity," unspoken but implicit, beckons once more.

Also numbered among my objectives in Chapter 5 is the task of showing what Sartre's commentators have too often neglected or only commented on in passing: How he used his historical reflections to address the long-standing debate between different types of nineteenth and twentieth century revolutionaries, notably Marxists and their anarchist adversaries. Throughout the nineteenth century and well into the twentieth, revolutionary and ideological politics were overwhelmingly anarchist in the "Latin" countries, Spain and Italy; whereas Germany's leftists, in marked and hostile contrast, were Marxists; and France was the country where both anarchists and Marxists flourished, engaged in endless battles, and also where various forms of anarchist/Marxist hybrids came to the fore, as in the thought of Georges Sorel—and, arguably, that of Jean-Paul Sartre.[4] The existing scholarship has much to say about Sartre's relationship to Marxism but virtually nothing to say about his relationship to anarchism, nor the various crossbreeds of anarcho-Marxism that were so common in France.

In the brief and final Chapter 6 ("History and a Note on Ethics"), we shall examine the hypothesis that, while ostensibly commenting on the French Revolution and Soviet history, Sartre, at times, came very close to injecting into his works a recapitulation of the history of social contract theory in reverse, moving from its most libertarian to its most authoritarian versions of consent, always allowing, however, for the possibility that the downtrodden will reach the moment when they can and must reassert their sovereignty.

Scholars have sought, with only modest success, for an implicit fulfillment in one or another of Sartre's works of his promise at the close of *Being and Nothingness* that he would soon offer an ethics. Or they have noted the prominence of the moral language of "authenticity" and "inauthenticity" in his immediate postwar essays, while conceding that he never converted those offerings into a full-fledged ethics.[5] Or they have underscored the revolutionary Sartre's dealings with the dilemma of means and ends in his plays and essays, *Dirty Hands, The Devil and the Good Lord,* and the introductory essay to Frantz Fanon's *The Wretched of the Earth.* In the end, they have often concluded that his ethics awaited the postrevolutionary society.

One other scholarly strategy has been to pore over Sartre's incomplete, fragmentary utterances on ethics in his final years.[6] Unnoticed is how close he came to working out a theory of a historically grounded, transmuting social contract in his discussion of revolution in motion, especially in the *Critique of Dialectical Reason*, where what he tried to pass off as phenomenological description verges on being something considerably more. It may be worth our while to take stock of what might have been but never was and to ponder why he refused to grasp what was readily at hand.

*   *   *

At the age of sixty-two, Sartre sat down for an interview during the course of which he remarked, "now I believe that only a historical approach can explain man."[7] He was not always so certain. How far he came, how fundamentally he changed his mind on the question whether "to historicize or not to historicize," can only be appreciated by revisiting *Nausea*, published at age thirty-three. Both chronologically and conceptually, Sartre's novel provides the baseline against which all his subsequent reflections on history must be judged. Revisiting *Nausea* is a necessary first step if we are to understand how he eventually rebuilt historical reason from the ashes of his attack on historians and historical knowledge in his remarkable novel.

Roquentin, the novel's protagonist, is a historian whose project it is to write a biography of the Marquis de Rollebon, a figure of the French Revolutionary era. Eventually Roquentin abandons that quest because he has concluded that history is useless: "When you want to understand something you stand in front of it, alone, without help: all the past in the world is of no use." In the course of encountering the absurdity of human existence, the contingency of our being, the strangeness of a natural universe to which we do not belong and in which we are *de trop*, out of place, and in the way, he finds that writing history is a futile and inexcusable escape. After abandoning his historical project he writes, "M. de Rollebon had delivered me from myself. What shall I do now?"[8]

It is all the worse that, unlike Roquentin, the contemptible bourgeois are more than willing to retreat relentlessly into the past. "They would like to make us believe that their past is not lost, that their memories are condensed, greatly transformed into Wisdom." Around the age of forty, "they christen their small obstinacies and a few proverbs with the name of experience." Roquentin concludes that "the past is a landowner's luxury" and soon thereafter jots a cautionary note in his diary: "Must not think too much about the value of History. One runs the risk of being disgusted."[9]

We are all storytellers, historians, novelists, whether we recognize it or not, remarks Roquentin. "A man is always a teller of tales, he lives surrounded by his stories [*histoires*] and the stories of others, he sees everything that happens to him through them; and he tries to live his own life as if he were telling a story." We are all historians, and all our histories are false because we read the present into the past. The good bourgeois "explain the new by the old—and the old by the older still, like those historians who turn Lenin into a Russian Robespierre, and a Robespierre into a French Cromwell." Desperately, we seek to convince ourselves that "there is nothing new under the sun."[10]

What's more, Roquentin the historian finds himself "beginning to believe that nothing can ever be proved." At most, he is offering "hypotheses," but these "come from me and are simply a way of unifying my own knowledge." History, Roquentin comes to believe, is more manufactured than recorded by the historian: "this feeling of adventure definitely does not come from events.... It's rather the way in which the moments are linked together"— and it is the historian who decides how to link them, what tale to tell, what lesson to be passed along to the reader.[11]

"I'd be better off writing a novel on the Marquis de Rollebon," decides Roquentin. "I have the feeling of doing a work of pure imagination. And I am certain that the characters in a novel would have a more genuine appearance." Everyone wants to believe in "true" stories, "as if there could possibly be true stories." You appear to start at the beginning, "and in reality you have started at the end." We immerse ourselves in someone's biography, address this or that moment in someone's life, and always "we forget that the future was not yet there." Truthful biography is not possible, nor is autobiography: "I wanted the moments of my life to follow and order themselves like those of a life remembered. You might as well try and catch time by the tail."[12]

To understand Sartre solely on the basis of his 1938 novel, one could not imagine that he would go on to write biographies of Baudelaire, Genet, and Flaubert, nor that he would pen his autobiography, *Words*. His future development as a thinker hinged on his success in turning a prewar repudiation of historical reason into a postwar critique of the same that would open the way to the ambitious historical writings that are central to his legacy.

✳   ✳   ✳

It was the experience of war that led Sartre to acknowledge his immersion in history and his social links to others. His life, as he acknowledged in 1975, was divided into "two almost completely distinct periods, ...: before the war and just after it."[13] During the war and because of the war, he experienced himself as a historical and social being, and this is what made it possible for him, after the war, to develop a historical method and an attendant social theory. To Simone de Beauvoir in October, 1939, he wrote that if he could "live and think this war on the horizon as a specific possibility of this era, then I would have grasped my *historicity*."[14] Dated February, 1940, an entry in his war diaries reads "*History* was present all round me."[15]

World War II dragged Sartre into history, and the same is true of his very special companion, Simone de Beauvoir. Much like Sartre, she wrote that "history took hold of me [in 1939], and never let go thereafter." "Suddenly," she added, "History burst over me," in spite of her previous self-admitted aversion to history.[16]

Again, it was the war that made Sartre and de Beauvoir question their philosophies of social isolation, which had been blocking the way to the development of the social theory that they would soon deem essential to historical reason. Roquentin wrote in his diary "I live alone, entirely alone," and declared that he had "no boss, no wife, no children; I exist, that's all."[17] Similarly, de Beauvoir, revisiting her youth, observed that she had "no husband, no children, no home," no social ties.[18] Speaking of herself and Sartre, she wrote "we belonged to no place or country, no class, profession, or generation."[19] Indifferent to public life, Roquentin, de Beauvoir, and Sartre never bothered to vote, not for the sake of protesting politically but out of disdain.[20]

Then came the war. It was the Nazi threat that prepared de Beauvoir for her later postwar reversal, her new-found recognition that "society has been all about me from the day of my birth; it is in the bosom of society, and in my own close relationship with it, that all my personal decisions must be formed."[21] She recognized the exact year of her transformation: "there is no doubt that the spring of 1939 marked a watershed in my life. I renounced my individualistic, antihumanist way of life. I learned the value of solidarity."[22]

For Sartre, too, 1939 was a turning point, the year when he acknowledged his ties to others while interacting with his fellows as a soldier and then as a prisoner of war. To de Beauvoir he wrote in 1939 of himself and his fellow soldiers that "a strange solidarity is developing among us, due neither to esteem nor to sympathy, but rather to our identical situations." Admittedly, he sometimes sounded another note, as when he sighed "I simply put up with them,"[23] but no sooner was he released than he suffered a sense of loss: "I had rejoined bourgeois society, where I would have to learn how to live once again 'at a respectful distance.' This sudden agoraphobia betrayed my vague feeling of regret for the collective life from which I had been forever severed."[24] Wistfully, Sartre in his final years recalled his experience as a prisoner: "In the stalag, I rediscovered a form of collective life I had not experienced since the École Normale." He had enjoyed "the feeling of being part of a mass."[25]

Ever willing to grant interviews in his later years and never one to hold back when asked about his past, Sartre commented that "before the war I thought of myself simply as an individual. I was not aware of any ties between my individual existence and the society in which I was living."[26] "After the war came the true experience, that of *society*."[27] It was his experiences during the war, especially his time in captivity, that disabused him of notions that he could exist outside society, on its fringes, relating to it only to express his contempt for all matters social. "One can only understand an individual, whoever he may be, by seeing him as a social being," he came to acknowledge. "But I did not discover that for myself until the war, and I did not truly understand it until 1945."[28]

* * *

It is not an accident that we have drawn upon the writings of Simone de Beauvoir to illuminate the moment when Sartre began to reconsider his aversion to history and society. Not only in regard to his early years but at every stage of his career, her testimony is always enlightening. Consequently, we shall frequently have recourse to her even though our focus will be on him. As she pointed out, her *Force of Circumstance* set forth "the entire chronicle of Sartre's political life up until '62."[29] No one, moreover, was better suited than de Beauvoir to comment on his reflections since her thought was his and his was hers. "We might almost be said to think in common," she wrote; "we have a common set of memories, knowledge, and images behind us; our attempts to grasp the world are undertaken with the same tools, set within the same framework, guided by the same touchstones."[30]

The support they afforded one another was forcefully attested by Sartre in a letter addressed to her near the beginning of his career: "In your last letter you explain how much I am *within* you. But you're *within me* too."[31] Interviewed by her near the end of his life, he affirmed "I had one special reader and that was you."[32]

* * *

Before World War II, Sartre gave his reasons, especially in *Nausea,* as to why he would not historicize. During the war, his personal experiences gave him reason to reconsider his original stand. After the war, he set out on a grand quest to historicize that would continue for the rest of his life—but not without complications and complexities.

Chapter 2

From Time to History

If time is central to history, Sartre left the door open in *Nausea* to a re-consideration of his position on history. For, in his novel, there are hints of what would be his preoccupation with time, five years later, in *Being and Nothingness*. When Roquentin observes a woman walking down the street, he asks, "do I *see* her motions, or do I *foresee* them? I can no longer distinguish present from future.... This is time, time laid bare." Later, he learns that his world is "the present, nothing but the present," that the past *was* but *is not*. Only the present *is*—the present fleeing into the future. In *Being and Nothingness,* Sartre would explain that it is the For-Itself, human consciousness, which introduces time into the dense, tenseless reality of Being-in-Itself.[1]

As everyone acknowledges, Martin Heidegger's *Being and Time* was the source of Sartre's treatment of temporal human reality. Less recognized, perhaps, is how often Sartre encountered in Heidegger's most famous book explicit references to and discussions of Wilhelm Dilthey,[2] who was a major figure of German historicist scholarship at the turn of the twentieth century and an intellectual whose interests in biography, textual interpretation, and related matters would soon become Sartre's. When Raymond Aron remarked that "Sartre in my view is the most Germanic of French philosophers,"[3] he had in mind his erstwhile friend's indebtedness to Husserl's phenomenology and Heidegger's ontology, of course, but also Dilthey's historicism.[4]

And so it was that as early as 1945, in an article written for *Les Temps Modernes,* Sartre displayed a burgeoning historical sensibility and a yearning for historical understanding. "Under the pressure of history we have learned that we are historical," he wrote. We have come to realize that our fate is to "live in history as fish do in water." What Cartesian mathematics was for the seventeenth century, Newtonian physics for the eighteenth century, and Lamarck's biology for the nineteenth, history must be for the twentieth century, Sartre wrote immediately after the war.[5]

Much to Sartre's chagrin was his discovery in 1945 that the more he immersed himself in historicism, the less possible it was to acquire the ultimate knowledge to which he aspired. "The more exquisite our historical awareness, the more we are irritated at floundering in the dark.... Is it not offensive that the secret of our era and the exact appreciation of our errors belong to individuals who have not yet been born?" At one and the same time Sartre accepted and chafed at the historicist view that the owl of Minerva only flies at dusk: we do not understand an era until it is over.

Sartre did not hesitate to admit that "the historian himself is a historical creature." Michelet and Taine were wrong to believe they could view history from the outside: "We are *inside.*"[6] In effect, Sartre was repeating Dilthey's view that historical knowledge is different in kind from the external knowledge of the natural scientist. The difference between Sartre and Dilthey is that while the latter man was willing to make peace with the limitations of historical knowledge, Sartre would always want something more. As a philosopher, phenomenology was not enough for Sartre; only a comprehensive ontology sufficed. As a historian, truths would not do; only Truth, one Truth, would satisfy him. This was true in 1945 and still true in 1960 when he published the first volume of the *Critique of Dialectical Reason.*

To establish Truth, he needed a method. From the 1940s onward, he searched for a method, conducting one experiment after another until he arrived, so he hoped, at his destination. The criticisms of historians enumerated in *Nausea* (see Chapter 1) were not forgotten; rather, they became object lessons in how not to write history, to be supplemented with lessons on how it should be written. Dilthey had thought of his work as a "Critique of Historical Reason";[7] similarly, after the war, Sartre sought to formulate a critique and reconstitution of historical reason that would prove superior, he hoped, to Dilthey's.

To retrace Sartre's journey toward history we must begin where he began, with his thoughts on the novel.

History and the Novel

In Sartre's universe, there is an intimate relationship between the writing of novels and the writing of history. It was in his novel *Nausea* that he made a case against history, and it was while writing about novels that he made many of his initial advances toward what amounted to an articulation of a histori-cist point of view, beginning in 1939 with a highly critical review of the novels of François Mauriac. Just as Monsieur Jourdain had been speaking prose all his life without knowing it, Sartre, consciously or not, was already speaking the language of historicism in 1939. A mere year after the publication of *Nausea,* Sartre was well on his way toward voicing a sophisticated historicist critique of a famous author's ahistorical technique of writing novels.

Whether accurately or not, Sartre accused Mauriac of omitting time and affirming "the novelist's divine lucidity" in his fiction. When Mauriac related events *sub specie aeternitatis,* "the novel disappears before your eyes." Much better was Ernest Hemingway, in whose novels "we hardly know the heroes except through their gestures and words." Mauriac's technique reeked of dogmatic religion and had been adopted in ignorance of science. "He takes God's standpoint on his characters" and fails to understand that "there is no more place for a privileged observer in a real novel than in the world of Einstein." In truth, "a novel is an action related from various points of view"; an omniscient narrator is a falsehood. "The participant's interpretations and explanations will all be conjectural. The reader ... will never get beyond the realm of likelihood and probability."[8]

Sartre's brief reference to Hemingway in 1939, along with short essays on Faulkner and Dos Passos in 1938 and 1939,[9] were the prelude to "American Novelists in French Eyes," published in *The Atlantic Monthly,* 1946. This latter essay was written in praise of Dos Passos, Faulkner, Hemingway, and other American novelists who had forged "a veritable revolution in the art of telling a story," a revolution transported to France where it "has produced a *technical* revolution among us." French writers "took from Faulkner the method of reflecting different aspects of the same event, through the mono-logues of different sensitivities."

Of the several American writers he mentioned, Dos Passos was likely the author who had the greatest influence on Sartre: "it was after reading a book by Dos Passos that I thought for the first time of weaving a novel out of various, simultaneous lives, with characters who pass each other by without ever knowing one another, and who all contribute to the atmosphere of a moment or a historical period." Dos Passos had shown that "one might describe a collective event by juxtaposing twenty individual and unrelated stories,"[10] and Sartre set out to do the same.

In an early essay, Sartre hailed Dos Passos as "the greatest writer of our time,"[11] and he applied the method of Dos Passos when writing his novel *The Reprieve* (1945), the second volume of *Roads to Freedom.* Mathieu, the main character, puzzled and frustrated, knows that the war is a major event but finds himself asking, "Where is it?" The war "takes and embraces everything," "it is everywhere ... but no one is there to add it up. It exists solely for God. But God does not exist."[12] A better summary of the viewpoint of German historicism, shorn of its original Hegelian religiosity, is difficult to imagine.

Simone de Beauvoir's position on the novel was close to Sartre's. "Only a novel, it seemed to me, could reveal the multiple and intricately spun meanings of the changed world to which I awoke in August 1944," she recalled two decades later. She added that "to convey the density of the world it is convenient to employ more than one point of view," as practiced in her own novels.[13] The original inspiration for her approach came from Dos Passos, Hemingway, and Faulkner, she stated in "An American Renaissance in France," an essay published in the *New York Times,* 1947.[14] No less important was her essay of 1946, "Literature and Metaphysics," in which she presented her finding that if existentialists frequently write fiction, it is because novels reconcile "the absolute and the relative, the timeless and the historical."[15] For both de Beauvoir and Sartre, the writing of "metaphysical novels" presented the opportunity to plunge deeply into the historical world without abandoning their grand metaphysical quest.

Although Sartre and de Beauvoir, when they looked back at the interwar period, championed the achievements of American rather than French novelists, that did not prevent them from appreciating the contributions of Saint-Exupéry. As early as his war diaries, Sartre noted with approval that "Saint-Exupéry's *Terre des Hommes* has a very Heideggerian ring to it."[16] Why Sartre was drawn to this particular novelist is perhaps best explained by de Beauvoir: "In describing the flier's world, Saint-Exupéry ... showed how diverse truths are made manifest by means of diverse techniques, yet each expresses the whole of reality, and no single one is privileged over the rest." Her conclusion was Sartre's as well: "it would have been hard," she wrote in her memoirs, "to conceive of a better, more concrete, or more convincing illustration of Heidegger's theories."[17] Sartre said in his diary that Heidegger had taught him "historicity" at the "very moment when war was about to make [this notion] indispensable to me"[18]; Saint-Exupéry, it seems, rendered those lessons unforgettable.

Later, in *What Is Literature?*, Sartre underscored some other reasons to praise Saint-Exupéry. By 1947, Sartre not only wanted to contemplate the world but he was "with those who want to change it." The airplane of Saint-Exupéry was "an organ of perception" and important as such, but it was also a tool, an example of how humans actively build their world. "Saint-Exupéry has opened the way for us." He is "the precursor of a literature of construction which tends to replace the literature of consumption."[19]

Roquentin in *Nausea* had explicitly chosen not to be "a man of action."[20] Samuel Beckett, dramatizing Sartre's original philosophy in *Waiting for Godot*, has one of his characters at the close of each act say "let's go," followed by the stage direction "they do not move." Sartre, following the war, made the opposite choice: "After Saint-Exupéry, after Hemingway, how could we dream of [merely] describing? We must plunge into action." *Undertakings* shall henceforth be our concern, "and all the undertakings we might speak of reduce themselves to a single one, that of *making history*."[21]

Sartre cared for Saint-Exupéry, but he cared even more for the American novelists, and the more he studied the writers on the other side of the Atlantic, the greater his fascination with the United States. In his comments on America, one sees that no matter how much he owed to Heidegger, Sartre also knew how to distance himself from his German predecessor. For if Heidegger's reactionary political outlook is evident in his comments on America, Sartre's embrace of modernity and focus on the future were on display whenever he looked across the ocean.

In Heidegger's estimation, America was a catastrophe. It was a country "that lacks completely any sense of history," whose people, rootless and overwhelmed by technology, unwilling to permit Being to disclose its mysteries, could not possibly be a *Volk* and might as well be Bolshevik.[22] By contrast, Sartre's America, before the Cold War embittered his view, was an enthralling land of skyscrapers, jazz, and innovative cinema; and its lack of history he regarded as the blessing of being released from the burden of the past. "We discovered skyscrapers with amazement in the films. They were the architecture of the future, just as the cinema was the art of the future and jazz the music of the future."[23] America was the present moving into the future.

Simone de Beauvoir recorded Sartre's excitement upon learning that he would visit America in 1945.[24] The articles he wrote at that time were, however, far from uncritical.[25] Like most European intellectuals, he lamented the shallow optimism of the Americans and their strange combination of individualism and social conformity: "it is public opinion that plays the role of policeman."[26] As a germinating leftist, he also regretted the lack of class consciousness in the ranks of the workers.[27] Nevertheless, he was attracted by the constant movement of Americans and fascinated by their cities that did not, as in Europe, represent the past. "The cities are open, open to the world, and to the future. This is what gives them their adventurous look and, even in their ugliness and disorder, a touching beauty."[28] Not even America's addiction to technology dampened Sartre's view. To the postwar generation "*doing* reveals *being*,"[29] which means that machines can be the fulfillment of Heidegger's quest instead of its nemesis.[30] Did not Saint-Exupéry's airplane reveal being?

American novels immersed Sartre in historicity. Visiting America taught him that historical thought, even if it begins with the past, is ultimately about the future. Only one thing more was needed, a method.

History as Existential Psychoanalysis

By 1943, Sartre had a method. In *Being and Nothingness* he had spelled out the scheme of "existential psychoanalysis" that he would employ later in his studies of Charles Baudelaire, Jean Genet, Gustave Flaubert, and arguably himself in his autobiography. Roquentin, be it recalled (Chapter 1), had decided that the biography he had undertaken was an exercise in futility: inevitably we falsify history by reading the present back into the past; better, then, to write fiction that calls itself fiction, concluded Roquentin, than to write fiction that calls itself biography. But a mere five years later, Sartre stepped forth with a method of helping a patient recapture his or her truthful history, or of helping the historian write an accurate history of a figure past (Baudelaire, Flaubert) or present (Genet).

Before setting forth his own kind of psychology, Sartre eliminated its competitors, behaviorism for one. John B. Watson had written that "behaviorism claims that 'consciousness' is neither a definable nor a usable concept; that it is merely another word for the 'soul' of more ancient times," to which he added that "no one has ever touched a soul, or has seen one in a test tube."[31] Sartre rejected Watson's efforts to turn psychology into a natural science, a study of external behavior only; he insisted as ardently as his German historicist predecessors on stressing human consciousness, even if consciousness figures as our curse in his first philosophy rather than our grandeur. Again like Dilthey and the German historicists, Sartre refused behaviorism's efforts to substitute causality for human freedom. The environment impinges on but does not determine us. Anguish is the "proof" of freedom.

It was Freud's psychology to which Sartre would turn but not before subjecting it, too, to a searching critique. All of Freud's grand theoretical constructs had to be purged: his famous division of the psyche into id, ego, and superego, for instance, which presented the human mind as if it were a thing, filled with things. A "mental struggle must be waged," Sartre argued as early as 1936, "in order to free ourselves from the almost unshakeable habit of conceiving all modes of existence as physical in type."[32] If Sartre in 1936 could not accept Husserl's "transcendental self,"[33] even less in 1943 could he sanction Freud's far less sophisticated philosophical assertions. It is our thoughts, our loves and fears, our encounters with the world that constitute our minds, not some transcendental box holding them; nor are we the *id* that occupies a central place in "the materialistic mythology of psychoanalysis."[34]

Behaviorism gets one thing right, but it is wrong even when it is right. Observing us from the outside, behaviorists quite correctly pay attention to our actions. Where they go wrong is in forcing the explanation of our actions into the framework of something like physiology. Stimulus-response is their favorite mode of explanation,[35] with the consequence that they fail to understand the meanings revealed by actions. "The nerve is not meaningful," wrote Sartre,[36] who insisted that our human world consists not simply of behavior but also of meaningful behavior.

Shorn of its grand theoretical pretensions, Freudianism is as rich a source of psychological understanding as behaviorism is a dead end. It is Freud's interpretive, historical method that is indispensable and that Sartre was eager to incorporate into existential psychoanalysis. "Both [Freudian and existential psychology] consider the human being as a perpetual, searching, historization."[37] We are our actions, our life, our history—and what we make of them. My actions over time reveal the self I have chosen to be, and with the assistance of my existential psychoanalyst, I can re-create a coherent and accurate account of my history.

There was a practical point to Freud's interpretive method much appreciated by Sartre, an objective of helping patients understand who they were, the better to seize control of their lives. A patient undergoing therapy could aspire, with the assistance of newly acquired self-knowledge, to become a more autonomous actor, still unhappy perhaps, but living on his or her own terms.

In common with Freud, Sartre maintained that "in each inclination, in each tendency the person expresses himself completely." The principle of existential psychoanalysis "is that man is a totality and not a collection.

Consequently he expresses himself as a whole in even his most insignificant behavior." And if this is so, then "we should discover in each attitude of the subject, meaning which transcends it." Up to this point, Freud and Sartre were in complete agreement.[38] Where they parted company was in Sartre's rejection of Freud's assurance that there is one set of symbols that the psychoanalyst can apply to all patients. Freud overstepped the bounds when he insisted, for example, that for all patients sticks, knives, and balloons symbolized the male; pits, cavities, and vessels the female.[39] "Our concern," wrote Sartre in disagreement with Freud, "is to understand what is *individual. ...* The method that has served for one subject will not necessarily be suitable for another subject or for the same subject at a later period."[40]

All current and previous psychologies, in Sartre's estimation, were guilty of treating the abstract as "prior to the concrete, and the concrete as only an organization of abstract qualities." The individual person disappears; "we can no longer find 'the one' to *whom* this or that experience has happened." Social psychologists miss the particular person when they speak of "the average adolescent," and Freud made a similar mistake when he spoke of my particular Oedipus complex as an instance of *the* Oedipus complex. Along the same lines, Sartre both in *Nausea* and in *Being and Nothingness* denounced historians who tried to explain the actions of an individual by citing a generic psychological trait such as "ambition." On this point, the difference between Sartre in 1938 and 1943 is that the later Sartre had at his disposal a method of interpreting why a particular person displayed ambition in a particular situation. During the war, Sartre decided that the merger of psychology and history could be successfully undertaken and that one need not follow Roquentin's example of abandoning it.[41]

Although Sartre agreed with Freud's therapeutic objective, he rejected Freud's claim that his therapy rendered conscious what had been unconscious. The notion that a "censor" suppresses certain of our urges, denying them admission to consciousness, is untenable. "How could the censor discern the impulses needing to be repressed without being conscious of discerning them?"[42] Sartrean psychoanalysis enables us to know that of which we are already conscious; it challenges us to stop living in "bad faith," making excuses rather than accepting responsibility for our actions.

However formidable Freud's accomplishments, he was also wrong to believe that psychoanalysis converts determinism into freedom. We were never determined; causality is irrelevant. "We shall never understand ourselves except as a choice in the making." Properly employed, psychoanalysis is the discipline by which we learn what free choice we made long ago about how to relate to the world, to others, and to ourselves. It unveils our "original choice," our "project," the "foundation" by which "all reasons come into being." Once we come into direct knowledge of our original choice, we are better equipped to comprehend who we were, who we are, and who we can be.[43] Humans have no nature; what they have is a history, and existential psychoanalysis is the tool that can enable them to recover their history—past, present, and potential future.[44]

*   *   *

Within a few years of its formulation, Sartre's version of psychoanalysis would begin to bear fruit as he initiated his ventures in writing biography. But the very first use of his new method came immediately in the form of a book review. On the French intellectual front, 1943 was noteworthy due to three interrelated events: It was the year that Gabriel Marcel coined the term "existentialism"; the year also when Sartre, having published *Being and Nothingness,* became identified with that label, which he eventually accepted; finally, and for our purposes most relevant, it was the year that Sartre published his review of Albert Camus's *The Stranger.* While Sartre praised Camus's novel, he also criticized it, by calling on the lessons in hermeneutics that he set forth in his philosophical treatise. In effect, Sartre used the section on existential psychoanalysis to make the case for why Camus's dramatization of the existential position was seriously flawed.

Sartre paid special attention to *The Stranger* because, as he remarked several years later, it was "the French novel which caused the greatest furor between 1940 and 1945."[45] To his liking was the success of Camus in "plunging us into 'the climate' of the absurd." Not at all to his liking, however, was Camus's presentation of his protagonist, Meursault, as if his status as an exemplar of existentialism were preformed, requiring no explanation, almost as if it were his essence. "His absurdity," commented Sartre, "seems to have been given rather than achieved; that's how he is, and that's that."[46]

Sartre would have us struggle to recognize that the past is past and to admit that the present fleeing into the future is all there is; Meursault, by contrast, without giving the matter any thought, simply announces, "I've always been far too much absorbed in the present moment, or the immediate future to think back."[47] Similarly, without thinking about it, Meursault knows that "one life was as good as another," a view that Sartre did not dare state until the end of nearly seven hundred pages of phenomenological ontology.[48] Again, while Sartre would train us to avoid losing the individual in an abstraction, Camus has his protagonist simply fail to understand that when the prosecutor speaks of "the prisoner's mistress," he means Marie. Likewise, Meursault finds a verdict rendered in the name of "the French people" incomprehensible.[49] What Sartre would take great pains to teach us, Meursault simply knows without knowing he knows.

To all appearances, Camus never realized the extent to which he had resorted to literary devices to concoct his incomprehensible protagonist. Dialogue is absent because "dialogue is the moment of explanation, of meaning, and to give it a place of honor would be to admit that meanings exist." By way of tenses of verbs, the French simple past, being the tense of continuity, was carefully avoided by Camus. Hemingway's style was mimicked for the reason that his clipped phrases misleadingly portray time as consisting of disconnected instants rather than as an organic unity.[50]

Nor is there ever any indication that Meursault suffered a crisis before the opening of *The Stranger* that would explain how he arrived at his outlook. It is only after he has been convicted and awaits execution that he self-consciously rebels. Until that late moment in the novel, the stranger has no idea that he is estranged.[51] The mind of the stranger is "so constructed as to be transparent to things and opaque to meanings," which is unacceptable because philosophy has "established the fact that meanings are part of the immediate data."[52] Camus's novel is fatally flawed insofar as its protagonist is presented as outside of history, impervious to hermeneutic understanding.

One other novel against which Sartre might have measured his newfound interpretive method, briefly mentioned in *What Is Literature?*,[53] is André Gide's *The Immoralist*. Like Roquentin, the protagonist Michel is a historian who, after suffering a personal crisis, stops being a historian. As he emerges from his illness, Gide's Michel undertakes a Nietzschean project of living beyond good and evil. His is a sustained exercise in sincerity; he peels away the layers of his socially acquired self, confident that underneath lies his true being.[54] "To thine own self be true" will henceforth be his implicit motto.

Nietzsche often figures in the pages of Sartre as he does in those of all the existentialists. But Sartre in *Being and Nothingness* had argued vigorously that I do not have a given self to which to be true. "What then is sincerity," he asked, "except precisely a phenomenon of bad faith?"[55] From a Sartrean perspective, Michel should have remained a historian so as to study the history of the self he had invented in the past and was struggling to reinvent in the present. He has no nature to recapture; he only has a history.

Neither the history spurned of Gide's immoralist, nor the history omitted of Camus's presentation of his amoralist is acceptable. Only by means of history can we understand ourselves or others.

History and Biography

In the section of *Being and Nothingness* devoted to existential psycho-analysis, Sartre set the stage for the writing of biographies, especially that of Flaubert, an undertaking that would be his obsession for three decades, not appearing until the early 1970s. Already in 1944 he was working on a soon-to-be-published study of Baudelaire,[56] and his biography of Genet would be published in 1952. The plan he employed while undertaking his biographical labors might be described as twofold: first, there was a recla-mation and updating of the insights of Dilthey and German historicism; second, there was Sartre's own distinctive but problematic contribution, drawn from his ontology.

Exactly as Dilthey had, Sartre insisted throughout his career that natural science should not be the model for studies of human history. The positivism of Comte, his search for a social science that would be a branch of natural science, is utterly wrong-headed. Whereas scientists search for natural uniformities, general laws, and causal relations, historians examine what is individual and beings who are free. Sartre's studies in Germany as a young man and his acquaintance with Raymond Aron's books on German sociol-ogy and philosophy of history were formative events of lasting significance in his intellectual life. From beginning to end, he shared the conviction of his historicist forebears that historical investigations were a search, difficult and demanding, not for causal explanation but for self-knowledge.

Much as Sartre would later, Dilthey had sought a rigorous method by means of which he could investigate the human subject, the unique indi-vidual, without falling into the trap of subjectivity—that is, without invoking mysterious and inexplicable intuition. Psychology, Dilthey surmised, was nec-essary for his purposes, but it had to be the study, not of timeless natural drives but of the subject's particular history.[57] Like the empiricists, Dilthey would be-gin with observation of an individual's external conduct, but unlike for Hume, the study of the external was for Dilthey only the first step of the investigation. "We are mainly aware of the inner life of others," wrote Dilthey, "only through the impact of their gestures, sounds and acts on our senses. We have to recon-struct the inner source of the signs which strike our senses."[58] Observation of action, conduct, behavior was the starting point; the real question, however, was what meaning was revealed over time by the doings of the subject. When Sartre's turn came, he followed exactly the same program of research.

"*Verstehen*," "understanding," "meaning," and "hermeneutics" were the words ever present in Dilthey's vocabulary. Understanding a human was, he held, more like interpreting a text than acquiring scientific knowledge of the physical world. It is because we, the historians, are part of the social and cultural world we study that we can understand the meanings of human actions. The "inside" of others is accessible because we, too, are "inside." Dilthey ambitiously believed his method of interpretive understanding provided "a vital link between philosophy and the historical disciplines, an essential part of the foundations of the studies of man."[59]

The list of similarities between Dilthey and Sartre is extensive. Dilthey had insisted that historians should study mind, which he deemed "an encompassing unity,"[60] much as Sartre would later speak of a person as a "totality." Biography (especially of Schleiermacher) was a special concern of Dilthey, as it would be for Sartre. Moreover, Dilthey insisted that "only by comparing myself to others and becoming conscious of how I differ from them can I experience my own individuality," much as Sartre would insist that a comparative method, "a comparative study of acts and attitudes," was necessary to decipher the meanings of the patient undergoing psychoanalysis.[61] Finally, just as Sartre with the help of Freud denied "privileged access" on the part of the patient to his or her psyche, Dilthey held that "the final goal of the hermeneutic procedure is to understand the author better than he understood himself."[62]

Clearly Dilthey and Sartre had much in common, but the differences also merit our attention. Dilthey would presumably have thought that some of Sartre's claims are excessive. Intellectually modest when necessary, Dilthey spoke of "the limits of all interpretation": it "can only fulfill its task to a degree; so all understanding always remains relative and can never be completed."[63] Standing in sharp contrast is the frequent demand of Sartre that the relative be complemented by the absolute;[64] also in contrast to Dilthey was Sartre's statement, late in life, that the point of his biography of Flaubert was to show that "one can manage to understand another man perfectly"; he would settle for nothing less than "to prove that every man is perfectly knowable as long as one uses the appropriate method."[65] Sartre's ambition for philosophy was always grand, too grand for the likes of Dilthey.

A related difference is that Dilthey shied away from ontology and was careful to avoid presenting the contrast between the study of natural science and human studies, *Naturwissenschaften* and *Geisteswissenschaften,* as if it hinged on a dualistic ontology. Sartre's ontology, of course, was dualistic, and he stated bluntly that "we should establish the goal of psychoanalysis from the standpoint of ontology."[66] Whether for better or for worse, Sartre's ontology figures prominently in his various biographical writings.

The method of existential psychoanalysis, as expounded by Sartre in *Being and Nothingness,* seeks to "reduce particular behavior patterns to fundamental relations—not of sexuality or of the will to power, but of *being.*" Once we have ascertained the subject's "project of being" our labors are at an end, not because of any limitations on our part but rather because we know everything; "for obviously it is impossible to advance any further than *being.*" Sartre's objectives are breathtaking—and they are worrisome; in his search for complete truth, he ran the risk of dogmatism. It is painfully obvious that at times his ontological claims leave a great deal to be desired, as when he said that women are "holes" in being, a blunder Simone de Beauvoir would have to correct (see Chapter 3). Everywhere in his biographical writings, the ontology of *Being and Nothingness* is present, but whether as instrument of discovery or as willful imposition is a difficult question to answer.[67]

*   *   *

From its opening pages, Sartre's biography of Baudelaire displays the resources of existential psychoanalysis. Somewhere around the age of seven, Sartre had postulated, was when a child makes the fundamental decision as to whom he or she would be. This was the moment of "original choice" of which he had spoken in *Being and Nothingness,* the foundation of the future self. In *Baudelaire,* Sartre placed his subject neatly, perhaps too neatly, into the conceptual scheme he had specified in his famous philosophical treatise.

At the age of seven, Baudelaire thought himself the center of the universe. His father had died when he was six, permitting him to believe he was in full possession of his mother, whom he adored. "It was precisely because he was completely absorbed in a being who appeared to be a necessary being … that he was shielded from any feeling of disquiet." He thought himself a "son by divine right." Then came his fall, when his mother remarried and he was sent off to boarding school. "The justification for his existence had disappeared; he made the mortifying discovery that … his life had been given him for nothing." As Sartre sees it, we confront the lessons of existentialism at a very early age.

Young Baudelaire was faced with "the shattering advent of self-consciousness." The story of his estrangement from his mother "brings us to the point at which Baudelaire chose the sort of person he would be."[68] What choice would he make, to embrace his freedom or to seek refuge in bad faith? Although Sartre paid little attention to Baudelaire the poet, author of *Les Fleurs du Mal,* he was very attentive to Baudelaire the man, whom he portrayed in the most damning light.

As re-created by Sartre, the life of Baudelaire was a ceaseless effort to escape from the human condition, especially from the knowledge that existence is gratuitous, superfluous, meaningless. Wanting to escape from the human condition entails wanting to escape from freedom, which is why "he tried all his life to *turn himself into a thing* in the eyes of other people and in his own." His "dearest wish" was to be like a stone or a statue. He wanted what is humanly impossible, to *be*. If "no one was farther from action than Baudelaire," that was because he did not wish to know he was perpetually obliged to form himself. Politically, he sided against George Sand and Victor Hugo because they "wanted to set men free."[69]

According to *Being and Nothingness,* it is our lot to struggle against "the Look" by which the "Other" seeks to turn us into objects. How perverse, then, was Baudelaire who craved "the pure 'external' look that would take him up and envelop him." This would be to return to childhood, a dream he never relinquished, anything to avoid assuming responsibility for his life. Baudelaire was "an eternal minor, a middle-aged adolescent who lived in constant rage and hatred, but under the vigilant and reassuring protection of others."[70]

Nowhere was Baudelaire more false, in Sartre's estimation, than in his refusal to accept the burden of creating values. When on occasion he bristled at the commands of his mother and stepfather, it was gleefully to flaunt his vices rather than to challenge their bourgeois virtues. The most banal of moralities he made his own, even as he indulged his taste for dandyism. He sided with the police and the judges who decided against him, rather than risk turning his rebellion-for-show into action that might change the world.[71]

Not least among Baudelaire's shortcomings was his view of history. In the nineteenth century, Marx, Michelet, Proudhon, and others, remarked Sartre, recognized that the future was what gave the present its meaning. "It is difficult today to realize the power of this great revolutionary and reformist current." Baudelaire, however, swam against the intellectual tide. For him, "it was the past which gave meaning to the present.... The old determined the new."[72] One need not shape the future if it was preformed by the past.

Such is Sartre's biography of Baudelaire, informed by his command of his subject's diaries and letters, argued by means of existential psychoanalysis, and without need of the postulate of the unconscious,[73] all in the service of proving that "bad faith" was the "besetting sin" of Baudelaire.[74] The unspoken but unmistakable moral of the story, of course, was that only the bourgeois society Sartre hated could have produced so hideous a genius as Baudelaire.

Sartre's biography of Jean Genet, *Saint Genet, Actor and Martyr* (1952), was in many respects the reverse image of his study of Baudelaire. In

Baudelaire's case, the "good people" of bourgeois society produced a pampered son and a literary figure whose most illicit thoughts were harmless exercises in art for art's sake; in Genet's, they fashioned a social outcast who employed the same powers of insidious, potentially subversive imagination to infect the minds of a crass bourgeoisie that did not know art but knew what it liked. Art for Baudelaire was fastidious social abdication; for Genet, it was unflinching revenge against respectable, proper society.

Both men were shaped at about age seven, but Baudelaire was ensconced in privilege whereas Genet was subjected to degradation; Baudelaire chose inauthenticity, Genet authenticity. Deserted by his mother, raised by foster parents, born in an urban setting but forced to live with peasants, Genet found himself surrounded by persons who valued property above all, while he was without property or prospects. To achieve being, he tried his hand at playing the saint, and when that failed, he stole trinkets to attain the property necessary for acceptance in a society dominated by property owners. Caught at the age of ten, called a thief, he made the momentous decision to treat theft as the signature event of his life: I shall be a thief!

"What is important," wrote Sartre, "is not what people make of us but what we ourselves make of what they have made of us." Genet accepted the socially constituted definition of himself as a criminal, a homosexual, a deviant, and yet eventually created great works of art. "I deeply admired this child who grimly *willed* himself at an age when *we* were merely playing the servile buffoon," wrote Sartre, sounding much as he would later in his self-deprecating autobiographical work, *Words*.[75]

Years later, both he and Simone de Beauvoir stipulated that the vindication of human freedom was the central theme of the biography of Genet. In 1969, Sartre remarked that "perhaps the book where I have best explained what I mean by freedom is *Saint Genet*"; it is freedom "which makes of Genet a poet when he had been rigorously conditioned to be a thief."[76] De Beauvoir added that "the whole basis of Genet's feeling for Sartre was this idea of liberty they shared, ... and their common abhorrence of all that stood in the way: nobility of soul, spiritual values, universal justice, and other such lofty words and principles, together with institutions or ideals."[77]

There are moments when Sartre successfully draws blood from the bourgeoisie in the course of writing Genet's biography. He is on target when he charges that "the sociologists of the French school" regard society "as the source of the sacred."[78] Emile Durkheim had said precisely that in his final book, in which he declared that "the idea of society is the soul of religion."[79] Elsewhere Durkheim had welcomed crime because it gives society an opportunity to reassert its collective norms against anyone who dares challenge them,[80] which made him a perfect target for Sartre. Unfortunately, Sartre could not let well enough alone. Not content with attacking the sociological defenders of the Third Republic, he spent much more time maintaining quite arbitrarily that the true spokesperson of the "good people" was Maurice Barrès,[81] a virulent right-wing opponent of the Third Republic.

Sartre's overindulgence of his ideological bent is not the only problem with his biography. His sprawling treatise abounds with references to "Being, Nonbeing, Nonbeing of Being and Being of Nonbeing."[82] Is Genet's person illuminated or lost, one may ask, in the constant barrage of Sartrean ontology? Also, in what sense did Genet rebel against bourgeois society when, on Sartre's not always consistent account, he knew neither as a boy nor as an adult that such was his project?[83] And where in Sartre's massive volume do we find a compelling explanation of why he thinks Genet's subversive imagination penetrated the minds of the bourgeois whereas Baudelaire's did not? Despite its extravagant length, Sartre's biography is unfinished business. It is not surprising that scholars have delivered sharply divergent verdicts on *Saint Genet*.[84]

*   *   *

Sartre's application of existential psychoanalysis was both brilliant and dogmatic. He was very effective at showing that his method could provide insights useful in answering the questions "Who am I?," "Who was Baudelaire?," "Who was Genet?" But he reached too far with his claims that his ontological categories offered definitive historical accounts of his subjects. In this regard, he might have learned something from one of his favorite predecessors, Nietzsche. Sartre was on firm footing when he dismissed Nietzsche's efforts to reduce our every undertaking to yet another assertion of the "will to power."[85] He was wrong, however, to omit Nietzsche's frank admission that his psychology was an interpretation, one among many. "Supposing," admitted Nietzsche, "that this also is only interpretation—and you will be eager enough to make this objection?—well, so much the better."[86]

There was one shortcoming Sartre did concede when in 1969 he reviewed his biographies of Baudelaire and Genet. By his own admission, his histories were hampered by the lack of fully realized social analysis. "The study of the conditioning of Genet at the level of institutions and of history is inadequate.... There was a whole context of his life that was missing."[87] His biography of Flaubert, he predicted, would overcome this shortcoming because post-1952 he had forged a social theory that would figure prominently in his last great historical work, *The Family Idiot*. Much had been accomplished through the good graces of existential psychoanalysis; even more would be within reach if existential psychoanalysis were complemented by a well-considered social theory.

History and Social Theory

Sartre's quest to write histories informed by a fully developed social theory culminated with the publication of *Question de Méthode*, translated as *Search for a Method*, and incorporated in 1960 into his *Critique of Dialectical Reason*. In 1971 and 1972, he at long last released the three volumes of his study of Flaubert, *The Family Idiot*, which was to be an application of his method and a final synthesis of his thought, a combination of the concepts and vocabularies of *Being and Nothingness* and *Critique of Dialectical Reason*.[88]

Commonly it is stated that it was Merleau-Ponty's sharp criticism in *Adventures of the Dialectic* (1955) of *The Communists and Peace* (1952–1954) that led Sartre to rethink his position and write the *Critique*. Deeply immersed in Marxism as well as phenomenology, Merleau-Ponty deemed Sartre's work woefully deficient in social and historical method. While there is much to be said for Merleau-Ponty's criticisms, it is worth noting that Sartre's search for a method began much earlier than 1955, dating back to the years immediately following the war. We have seen that the experience of war introduced him to historical consciousness; the same point may be made about social consciousness: "I received a mobilization slip.... This was what made the social aspect enter my mind. I suddenly understood that I was a social being."[89]

Sartre made brief but significant contributions to social theory when he penned an introductory essay to *Les Temps Modernes* in 1945, followed a year later by additional thoughts on social theory in *Anti-Semite and Jew*. Sartre's contribution in these works came in the form of his contention that liberals and their eighteenth-century predecessors, the philosophes, failed to understand our social ties, whereas the right-wing ideologues of his day incorrectly turned our group memberships into an essence, Marxism alone comprehending both that we are group beings and that the relationships within and between groups change over time.

Liberals, he held, look upon persons "as mosaics in which each stone coexists with the others without that coexistence affecting the nature of the whole." Jews need to have their rights as a group protected but that will not happen if good liberals decide the matter, since liberals recognize "neither

Jew, nor Arab, nor Negro, nor bourgeois, nor worker, but only man—man always the same in all times and all places." The method of the liberals is "analytic," which "excludes the perception of collective realities." To a liberal, "a social body" is nothing more than "a collection of individuals."[90]

The right-wingers, by contrast, employ a "synthetic" method. Sartre, now convinced that we are not just individuals but "social individuals," approved the right-wingers' contention that the whole is more than the sum of its parts. What he could not abide was their insistence that social identities are simply given rather than historically acquired. To be French, for them, is to congratulate oneself on enjoying a Gallic essence; nothing need be done to earn one's sense of achievement. Likewise, "for the anti-Semite, what makes the Jew is the presence in him of 'Jewishness.'"[91]

Marxism in Sartre's estimation stood alone in that it was both synthetic and historical in its method. To their credit, Marxists characterized the bourgeois on the basis of their behavior, not their nature. They allowed for the possibility that some members of the bourgeoisie will break away from their social class and join the proletariat in its struggle, in which case "they will be judged by their acts, not by their essence."[92] Historical and sociological, Marxism sought the explanations of class formation and class conflict that eluded both liberals and those who gathered under the banner of "true France."

There can be no doubt that Sartre did make advances toward the development of social theory in his essays of 1945 and 1946. It is also clear that he sometimes wore Marxist blinders, as when he stated that "we find scarcely any anti-Semitism among workers."[93] Another deficiency was that Sartre's understanding of the Enlightenment and nineteenth-century liberalism was frequently little more than a caricature cribbed from vulgar Marxists and Enlightenment-bashing right-wingers. He missed the complex discussion in the ranks of the philosophes concerning when the analytical method is appropriate and when not.[94] No less misleading was his claim that the philosophes professed belief in an unchanging human nature, when in fact they drew from Locke's *tabula rasa* precisely the opposite lesson—that we are individually and collectively historical beings.[95] As for his complaint that the members of the Third Estate sought their revolutionary goals by "abdicating their class consciousness,"[96] it could only be lodged by ignoring Sieyès' radical *What is the Third Estate?*. And his attribution of an ahistorical philosophy to nineteenth-century liberals required that he overlook their project of deradicalizing Sieyès by writing histories of the slow, evolutionary, progressive march of the Third Estate throughout the centuries, from the burghers of medieval cities to the nineteenth-century bourgeoisie.[97]

Throughout the 1940s, Sartre was still finding his way with Marxism. He could successfully criticize the Communist party's philosophy in "Materialism and Revolution" (1946), its addiction to a determinism that was metaphysical and inconsistent with its call to action; but when it came to applying Marxism in publications such as *Anti-Semite and Jew,* he was far too schematic and formulaic. Over the next decade he would hone his skills as a Marxist thinker, his moment of triumph arriving with *Search for a Method.* By 1957, he was ready to step forth with a Marxism that was supple and well suited to work in tandem with existential psychoanalysis.

Against French Communists, Sartre appealed to Marx himself in *Search for a Method,* the Marx who wrote *The Eighteenth Brumaire of Louis Bonaparte,* in which he acknowledged the complexity of class figuration at midcentury rather than imposing on France the bipolarized scheme of his *Communist Manifesto.* The Marx who matters is the one who refrained from imposing a formula upon the whole of history, limiting himself instead to the task of dealing with the dynamics of nineteenth-century capitalism or the history of earlier times from the perspective of what led to the rise of capitalism. Sartre also lauded Marx for attempting "a difficult synthesis of intention and of result."[98] Not at all, then, did Sartre's Marx concede to German idealists sole use of the method of *Verstehen,* although his Marx did insist that it was only one element of a satisfactory treatment of history.

While Sartre sometimes assaulted vulgar Marxists by citing Marx, his more characteristic maneuver in *Search for a Method* was to inject revised German historicism into rigid contemporary Marxism. They are Sartre's words but might as well be Dilthey's when we read "What we call freedom is the irreducibility of the cultural order to the natural order."[99] All through his treatise, Sartre sharply distinguished the method of historical science from that of natural science; tirelessly he upbraided Marxist positivism, condemned its determinism, its reductionism, its habitual absorption of the concrete event and the individual person into an abstract universalization.[100] Historical writing could only succeed if it followed a rigorous program of "experiment, observation, phenomenological description, understanding, and specialized works."[101]

Possibly Sartre's single greatest affinity with German historicism came in his discussion of the method of "comprehension," which was strikingly similar to Dilthey's *Verstehen.* "To grasp the meaning of any human conduct," wrote Sartre, "it is necessary to have at our disposal what German psychiatrists and historians have called 'comprehension.'" Contemporary Marxism, having refused to investigate significations, fails miserably because "man is, for himself and for others, a signifying being." Signs reveal who we are, our projects, our movement beyond the present into a new future, whereas the Party's theoreticians understand the new as a mere restatement of the old—they explain the Hungarian uprising of 1956, for example, as a replay of the actions of the counter-revolutionaries of 1793.[102]

Recovering the meaning of human projects was only one facet of historical investigation. We must also recognize that "one of the most striking characteristics of our time is the fact that history is made without self-awareness." That is to say, history is a record of unanticipated consequences, "of acts with no author, of constructions without a constructor."[103] Beyond individuals are the social structures in which they are trapped, the collective forces that "await us from birth" and explain how it is that "we are all lost during childhood."[104] Sartre went so far in his *Critique* as to reach out to the publications of structuralist Claude Lévi-Strauss—but without abandoning his anti-structuralist premise that all historical accounts must begin with the individual human subject.[105]

For Sartre, the human subject was always the starting point and human freedom always the foremost concern. But the more he immersed himself in social theory, the less he could hold on to his original assertions about freedom. If at first he was adamant that under any and all circumstances we are free, the later Sartre mocked his earlier stand: "it's incredible, I actually believed that!" Eventually Sartre came around to the view that freedom was to be regarded as especially precious because it is so rare. "This is the limit I would today accord to freedom: the small movement which makes of a totally conditioned social being someone who does not render back completely what his conditioning has given him."[106]

*   *   *

Search for a Method, Critique of Dialectical Reason, and *The Family Idiot* were the texts where Sartre's initial antisocial, anti-historical views went to die, and where his eventual social and historical outlook went to ripen. The familiar sociological concepts of social "functions" and social "roles" are exemplary cases of the progressive maturation of Sartre's social theory— concepts reborn in his later historical writings after having been mocked and ridiculed during his earlier years.

Roquentin vigorously dismisses all claims that the notion of "function" is of explanatory value. "The world of explanations and reason is not the world of existence," he notes in his diary, and soon makes his argument more explicit by pointing out that the concept of function does not help him understand the root of a tree. "The function explained nothing: it allowed you to understand generally that it was a root, but not *that one* at all. This root, with its color, shape, its congealed movement, was ... below all explanation." How much more must this be true of a human being, if it is true of an object in nature: the existent is lost in the concept.

Nevertheless, immediately after the war we find Sartre speaking with keen interest about "the social function" of literature. Through the back door, the sociological concept of "function" had entered his thought, and by 1960, he welcomed it through the front door. In the *Critique of Dialectical Reason,* he spoke at length about the moment when a group, to save itself, enters the stage of "organization." When this happens, there is a distribution of tasks, a differentiation of functions, and a given individual is obliged to educate him- or herself to assume the attendant tasks.[107]

Social functions imply social roles, so when Sartre rehabilitated the former he also granted belated respectability to the latter. This reversal, however, was a long time coming. Both in his novel and in his grand philosophical treatise, his comments on social roles were caustic. "*Nausea* is the literary culmination of the 'man alone' theory," Sartre commented in his final years, and he also admitted "I *was* Roquentin."[108] That is, the early Sartre was as one with the protagonist of his novel who, visiting a park, sees a man making programmed gestures in the presence of his child to convince himself that he is "nothing but a father." All the bourgeois are the same, immersed in everyday routine, playing their roles to delude themselves into thinking that "the world obeys fixed, unchangeable laws."[109] Apparently Sartre at the beginning of his career adamantly refused to admit the sociological concept of social roles to his thought.

In *Being and Nothingness,* Sartre did reluctantly grant that there were social roles, but placed them under the rubric of "bad faith." The waiter wants to be a waiter as a table is a table; he wants *to be.* "There is the dance of the grocer, of the tailor, of the auctioneer, by which they endeavor to persuade their clientele [and themselves] that they are nothing but a grocer, an auctioneer, a tailor." Their typical gestures and mechanical actions are evasions of freedom and responsibility. "Yet there is no doubt that I *am* in a sense a café waiter.... But if I am one, this can not be in the mode of being-in-itself. I am a waiter in the mode of *being what I am not.*" Against the backdrop of his early novel and philosophical treatise, one can appreciate how far Sartre had to travel before arriving at his firm embrace of the concept of social roles and functions in *Search for a Method* and the *Critique*.[110]

Another measure of how far Sartre's thought had evolved, and why it changed, is his total reversal of his initial stand on social isolation. Prior to 1939, he said he "had no political opinions" and thought of himself as an individual "who owes nothing to society and whom society cannot affect."[111] To isolate oneself from society was a solution because it allowed Roquentin or Sartre to live on his own terms. In 1944, even as he embraced the Resistance movement, he continued to evade social ties: membership in the Resistance, in his account, was characterized as an experience of belonging to a group while remaining "alone" and in "solitude."[112]

After he became thoroughly politicized, Sartre could no longer accept such uncompromisingly asocial views; the isolation that prevented individuals from fusing into a group for the purpose of changing society was something he had come to bemoan. Hence the passages of the *Critique* in which he exposes how modern society manufactures isolation and political impotence. Waiting for the bus, we hide behind our newspapers because such is our socialization; similarly, a city "is present in each one of its streets *insofar as it is always elsewhere*"; and impotence is the bond of the free market. Isolation is socially created rather than given, problem rather than solution. Social theory, he had come to believe, is needed to explain the absence of social relations and the consequential disabilities of revolutionary politics.[113]

*   *   *

The aim of the first *Critique of Dialectical Reason* was to prepare the way for the writing of history; it included historical examples but was not itself a history.[114] For that, we must turn to *The Family Idiot,* where Sartre drew together many of the strands of his previous work and attempted to weave them into a fulfillment of all he had learned over the years from his many encounters with history.

One example of his efforts in *The Family Idiot* to draw on his earlier thought even as he set forth his mature reflections is his renewed focus on the relationship between the novel and history. He had begun by having Roquentin abandon history to write a novel because history is never true, never more than an exercise in imagination. His study of Flaubert returns to but revises the stand he had taken in *Nausea*. We still find him saying "I would like my study to be read as a novel," but he hastened to add that "it is a *true* novel," true because "I used what I think were rigorous methods." Imagination itself, if properly employed, can be an effective method. The documents Flaubert left behind are plentiful, but where there are gaps Sartre filled in the blanks by resorting without embarrassment to imagination. Conjecture, hypothesis—or imagination—are essential ingredients of discovery; Roquentin foolishly discarded them because they were not directly dictated by the data, Sartre at a later date came to their rescue.[115]

With a combination of conjecture and empathy borrowed from his earlier thoughts on existential psychoanalysis, Sartre sought entrance into Flaubert's inner world. What he discovered was the passivity of his subject, a topic that escaped Freudian but not existential psychoanalysis.[116] The mother, he speculated, wanted a girl and expressed her disappointment by attending to her boy dutifully but without love. The father doted on the first son, Achille, but neglected Gustave, inferior because second in birth order and whose difficulties learning to read might mean that he was destined to be "the family idiot." Unloved, Gustave could not love himself or anyone else. Emotionally deprived, passive because uncertain of himself, faring poorly in the world of the real, he was prepared at an early age to seek refuge in the imaginary.

Unfortunately, Gustave's cherished role of writer did not fit well with the bourgeois preoccupations of his father. As a young man, Gustave was at odds with the head of the household, but did not think highly enough of himself to rebel; it was unthinkable that he should reject the career that had been chosen for him. What he could do, but without admitting this to himself, was suffer a mysterious physical breakdown in 1844. Sartre argued forcefully that neither epilepsy nor any other physical explanation is convincing. No, Gustave's wounds were willed, self-inflicted, "intentional,"[117] the product of a neurosis, perhaps, but one chosen by Gustave so that he might be set free to write rather than practice law.

Throughout his account Sartre integrated existential psychoanalysis with historical sociology, in fulfillment of the research design adumbrated in *Search for a Method.* Here, as everywhere, class analysis was central to Sartre's sociology. At considerable length, he related the story of the Flaubert family: the bourgeois father, well to do but not well enough to be accepted in high society; the mother with her vaguely aristocratic heritage; the first son who would follow and vindicate the career of the father. Then there was Gustave, hopelessly bourgeois but ever yearning for the recognition of aristocrats, eventually the man of the Second Empire, never the man of the mediocre Third Republic. Comfortable at Louis Napoleon's court under the protection of Princess Mathilde, Flaubert was convinced that the Franco-Prussian War, the "mad dogs" of the Paris Commune, and the advent of the Third Republic had consigned him to the ranks of the "living dead."[118]

In the third volume of *The Family Idiot*, Sartre rejoined his much earlier effort in *What Is Literature?* to study the literary movements of previous centuries and the relationship between writer and public. The difference, of course, was that he now had at his disposal the social theory that was largely missing in 1947 but had come to fruition with the publication of the *Critique of Dialectical Reason*. Flaubert came into focus in the final volume of Sartre's study against the backdrop of the Romantic and Post-Romantic literary styles, and these, in turn, were to be understood in their relationship to the social order of the day.

What, Sartre asked, was the cultural world of Flaubert and others who were coming of age in the 1840s? For their parents, Voltaire was not yet irrelevant, but for the children, it was the Romantics of the early nineteenth century who mattered, figures such as Victor Hugo. Sartre had little sympathy for the Romantic adoration of the emotions because he had always believed that our emotions are of our own making, that sadness, for instance, is a "conduct," a cup we must remember to refill, and he contended that appeals to the emotions are acts of bad faith.[119] Similarly, as opposed to the unqualified enthusiasm of the Romantics for "imagination," Sartre countered with the mixed report that the imaginary is both the proof of our freedom and also an invitation to escape from the real—an escape, too, as was true of the emotions, from responsibility. This much, however, Sartre was willing to say in behalf of the Romantics who appealed to the emotions and imagination: that they frequently did so to plunge into human affairs and fight the good fight.

With the transition from the Romantics to the Post-Romantics, what he spied was that the art, emotion, and imagination of the earlier generation that would transform the world degenerated into the art for art's sake that would secede from the real into the imaginary. Flaubert (and Baudelaire) prepared the way for Mallarmé, Parnassus, Symbolism, the art and poetry of the last quarter of the nineteenth century. These were the "Knights of Nothingness" who, hating humanity, deliberately made of art something inhuman. Flaubert, "the Lord of Nonbeing" and "the Prince of the Imaginary,"[120] loathing himself and therefore the world, had shown the way. His neurosis, which was ahead of his age, was to become a collective neurosis.

Unlike previous artists, the Knights of Nothingness chose to obliterate the ties between writers and public. And yet Flaubert and his coterie had not succeeded in cutting themselves off from the larger society. Their works were well received in spite of themselves, and Sartre believed he knew why. All the good bourgeois were guilty of betraying their ideals in 1848; all approved the violent suppression of the workers. Afterward, "the bourgeoisie surrendered to the Emperor out of fear, out of hatred of man, because its experience in '48 taught it that the social order can be maintained only by repression."[121] Flaubert and the Knights of Nothingness shared with the reigning bourgeoisie a hatred of everything human.

In spite of the contempt of Post-Romantic authors for the public, the match between the cynicism and inhumanity of the writers and that of their privileged readers was perfect. Flaubert's understanding of his social position was entirely off the mark. Mistakenly he believed he had succeeded in using imagination to derealize and escape from the real when, in fact, he had invited the conclusion that whatever is, is right. What, then, could be more fitting and ironic than for the public, seeing the truth of their vicious and predatory world in his art, pin on him the label he would have deemed most abhorrent, that of "realist?"

Problems and Possible Solutions

Did Sartre violate his historicism when he announced that he would settle for nothing less than "*one* human history, with *one* truth?"[122] Again, did he violate it by imposing his ontological categories upon the subjects of his investigations? Did he go well beyond what any good historicist should strive to achieve?

Perhaps he did use and abuse his ontological categories in his biographies of Baudelaire and Genet; perhaps he was sometimes guilty of ontological reductionism. In his own fashion, he may have been as dogmatic in imposing his philosophy as Freud was in imposing his sexual categories. Even so, in the culminating study of Flaubert, he did not force cultural history to yield to ontology; if anything, we encounter precisely the opposite, ontology reduced to cultural history. Everywhere in the third volume is the language of being and nothingness, but now it is Flaubert, Mallarmé, and the Symbolists who speak such language in their own voices, for their own purposes. They are the Knights of Nothingness, electing to opt out of the bourgeois society of their day in which they are nevertheless deeply embroiled. Falsely, they convince themselves that their wrongdoing is "*ontological* culpability,"[123] that they could do no other because such is the nature of Being and Nothingness.

As for the talk of one history and one truth instead of many, Sartre's position need not be as dogmatic as it sounds, and perhaps sometimes is. To his credit, he never wavered from his stand in *Being and Nothingness* that "the historian is himself historical."[124] No point of view on the totality is conceivable; truth is a becoming, history a totality in the making, each totality detotalized and open to future development. Sartre's point was that the historian's calling is to unite theory with *praxis*. History lies ahead, not behind us. "Our historical task," he wrote in *Search for a Method*, "is to bring closer the moment when History will have *only one meaning*," forged by political revolution.[125]

The Truth of History, for Sartre, is not waiting to be discovered but comes to be, which can only happen if we make it happen. In our day, he believed, history is becoming universal history as different parts of the world are increasingly tied to one another.[126] History is becoming One and that one will be true if and when humanity experiences the triumph of revolution.[127]

Chapter 3

The Historical Search for the Unhistorical

On the topic of history, not one but two Sartres emerged from the Occupation and Resistance. First, there was the Sartre we have already encountered, the writer who, having abandoned his prewar claim that history was untrue and beside the point, eventually advanced so far as to hold that there is a universally true history and that historians wielding the proper methodology have it within their power to answer definitively such difficult questions as "Who was Flaubert?" and "Who am I?"

Then there was a second Sartre who stepped forth after the war, a figure who outspokenly espoused a historical point of view, but nevertheless fixated on groups he believed were denied a history: the French during the Occupation, Jews throughout the centuries, the French proletariat of the early 1950s, colonized peoples in Algeria and elsewhere, Cubans before their Revolution, and—Simone de Beauvoir added—women. "Slaves, serfs, workers" are numbered among the "nonhistorical elements" of society, Sartre wrote in 1947. "History takes place beyond them."[1]

Sartre constantly was on the lookout for groups trapped in extreme situations, victimized by society, removed from the flow of history, and forced to choose between heroic defiance and abject capitulation. From the moment humans have the possibility of a future, they usually choose to lose themselves in the past. They become inauthentic. Hence Sartre was always ambivalent about history and fascinated by those groups that history had deserted, leaving them stranded in a static present.

Historicism itself sanctioned this escape clause from the processes of history. Hegel had pointed to a modern society, America, and denied that its inhabitants were a historical people. Lacking the social differentiation that comes with the passage of time, marked more by space than time, not governed by a State, the Americans were noteworthy but not yet historical.[2] Sartre exploited this opening for non-historicity within historicism for his own existentialist purposes. In his eyes, there was no lack of groups that stood outside history in his own day. Authenticity was what he initially hoped to discover within their ranks; later, he sought agents of revolution who would transfigure their non-history into the future as history.

Resistance and Refusal

It was during the Occupation that Sartre first discovered a people—none other than his compatriots—who had experienced a stoppage of history. "For four years our future had been stolen from us," he observed shortly after the war ended. Looking back, he noted that "at each instant we sensed that a link with the past had been crushed; traditions had been broken."[3] How terrible those years had been but also how admirably some members of the Resistance had risen to the occasion were his concerns in "The Republic of Silence," originally published in 1944.

The Sartre whose alter ego was the purposeless Roquentin makes no appearance in the forceful passages of "The Republic of Silence." Nor is there room for the man who had ended *Being and Nothingness,* a mere year earlier, with the shocking claim that "it amounts to the same thing whether one gets drunk alone or is a leader of nations."[4] Instead, the reader is treated to a dramatic account of humans living in devastated space and frozen time, some of whom transformed their bleak, desperate circumstances into a remarkable tribute to all that is most noble: "Exile, captivity, and especially death (which we skillfully hide from ourselves in happy times) became for us the perpetual objects of our cares. We learned that . . . it was necessary to see in them our *lot,* our destiny, the profound source of our reality as men."[5]

Curiously, Sartre began his essay by saying "never were we more free than during the German occupation." The French suffered arbitrary deportation, daily insults, and lost their rights, and "because of all this, we were free." Sartre's view was reminiscent of and yet quite different from his stand in

Being and Nothingness. For although he had maintained in his philosophical tome that when tortured we are still free to decide at what moment to capitulate, he had not said that torture makes us especially free.[6]

Perhaps the expression Sartre should have uttered was not "freedom" but "authenticity." His comments certainly invite such a conclusion: "the choice that each of us made of himself was an authentic choice because it was made in the presence of death." If, as he held in his earliest writings, it is our ties to others that open the door to inauthenticity, then membership in the Resistance was, of all possible collective affiliations, the perfect choice because it allowed one to belong to a group and yet to live in solitude. The members of the Resistance "did not fight out in the open like soldiers. They were hunted down in solitude, arrested in solitude. It was completely abandoned and destitute that they held out against torture, alone and naked in the presence of the torturers.... Yet, in the depths of their solitude, it was the others they were protecting, all the others, all their comrades in the Resistance."

Resistance fighters experienced "total responsibility in total solitude," and their organization suggested the outlines of the best possible republic. "For the leaders and for the rank-and-file ... the punishment was the same—imprisonment, deportation, death. There is no army in the world where there is such an equality of risk for the soldier and the generalissimo. And this is why the Resistance was a true democracy"—and a moment in which to be committed, responsible, and authentic were one and the same.

Lurking behind Sartre's essay on the years when France was isolated from history, one can sometimes detect the shadowy but discernible figures of previous philosophers. Nietzsche is frequently mentioned in Sartre's writings, and it is arguable that in "The Republic of Silence" Sartre stood Nietzsche on his head. "All truly noble morality grows out of triumphant self-affirmation," wrote Nietzsche. "Slave ethics, on the other hand, ... begins by saying No to an 'outside,' an 'other,' a non-self.... All its action is reaction."[7] Unlike Nietzsche, Sartre sided with the "slave." In "The Republic of Silence," he congratulated "all Frenchmen who, at every hour of the night and day throughout four years, answered NO." Both Nietzsche and Sartre reformulated Hegel's famous phenomenology of Master and Slave, Nietzsche siding with the master, Sartre with the slave because in the worst times of the modern world one is far more likely to find authenticity and nobility among the slaves than the masters.

The Stoics and Descartes are the other philosophers who flitter in the background of Sartre's essay on the Resistance. "I have always had sympathy for the Stoics,"[8] Sartre remarked in his final years, and Simone de Beauvoir repeatedly commented on his fascination with the Stoics.[9] What the fixation on the Stoics illuminates is Sartre's strange insistence in "The Republic of Silence" that we are free even when in chains. "Take me and cast me where you will," wrote Marcus Aurelius; "I shall still be the possessor of [myself]."[10] Epictetus, the Stoic as slave, said the same. At this moment in his career, Sartre agreed. Under the worst of circumstances, we are still free to say yes or no, to resist and die or to capitulate and live.

Descartes had taught much the same lesson: "My ... maxim," he wrote, "was to try always to conquer myself rather than fortune, and to alter my desires rather than change the order of the world, and generally to accustom myself to believe that there is nothing entirely within our power but our own thoughts."[11] Following in the footsteps of his formidable predecessor, we find Sartre saying, "Descartes has here made, after the Stoics, an essential distinction between liberty and power. To be free is not to be able to do what one wants but to want what one can."[12]

Sartre summoned all the resources of the philosophical tradition to laud those who resisted when faced with their removal from history by the forces of evil. For the victims of the Nazis, there was no past to which to retreat, and that, however strange, was their great advantage.

The Timeless Plight of the Jews

In none of his writings does Sartre strive more diligently to portray a people living outside history than in *Anti-Semite and Jew* (1946). Not coincidentally, nowhere else does he offer an argument that hinges so strongly on the notions of authenticity and inauthenticity.

Admittedly, in *Being and Nothingness*, he had objected to the presence of the words "authenticity" and "inauthenticity" in Heidegger's vocabulary, "because of their implicit moral content."[13] It is also true that his essay on the Jews contains one lonely parenthetical assertion that the designation "'inauthentic' implies no moral blame."[14] Nevertheless, it is impossible to read his polemic without acknowledging from the first page to the last the constant presence of those two words, always invoked to praise the authentic and condemn the inauthentic life. Neither can we miss that it is, to his mind, the non-historicity of the Jews that sharply poses for them the choice between authenticity and inauthenticity; nor that the claims of historical rootedness on the part of the anti-Semites are central to their unbudging and despicable inauthenticity.

No one, he assures us, is more inauthentic than the anti-Semite; no one more fearful of his freedom or more eager to turn himself into a thing. Anti-Semites "are people attracted by the durability of a stone. They wish to be massive and impenetrable." The anti-Semite is "a man who wishes to be pitiless stone …—anything except a man." He "flees responsibility …, and choosing for his personality the permanence of rock, he chooses for his morality a scale of petrified values."[15] A better example of a person living in "bad faith" cannot be found than the anti-Semite, for it is not without difficulty that the anti-Semite fails to note that he "*chooses* the permanence and impenetrability of stone." Although "anti-Semitism is a free and total choice of oneself," the anti-Semite adamantly insists that choice has nothing to do with his conduct.[16]

To suffocate themselves in false certainties and to hide from themselves responsibility for their actions, anti-Semites capitulate to their emotions, especially anger. In his philosophical writings dealing with the emotions, Sartre had concluded that our emotions do not overwhelm us, as we wish to believe; rather, we choose to be overwhelmed by our emotions. Emotions are our excuses, our way of evading responsibility for our actions. Anger, for instance, is simply "an escape,"[17] he had written in 1939. Later, while writing his essay on "the Jewish question," Sartre carried his original phenomeno-logical findings into the realm of political controversy: anti-Semitism, he affirmed, is a choice to capitulate to our emotions, anger most notably. What the anti-Semite does not wish to know is that "we must always *consent* to anger before it can manifest itself." Only a "strong emotional bias can give us a lightning-like certainty; it alone can remain impervious to experience and last for a whole lifetime."[18]

Throughout his essay on Jews and Anti-Semites, Sartre repeatedly took what had been a universal statement in *Being and Nothingness* and transformed it into a specific and political proposition. All of us, the great philosopher of ontology had stated in 1943, wish to delude ourselves into thinking we possess an essence, and in 1946, the philosopher turned engaged journalist made the same point when speaking about those who live to hate Jews. "There is nothing I have to do to merit my superiority, and neither can I lose it. It is given once and for all."[19] One is born an Aryan and that's all there is to it. It is my essence.

Similarly, Sartre had argued in his grand philosophical treatise that all of us are tempted to deny our freedom and the burdens it entails. In 1946, he applies that same lesson to the Nazis and their sympathizers: "The anti-Semite is afraid of discovering … that man … [is] the master of his destinies, burdened with an agonizing and infinite responsibility."[20] He flees from his freedom and from himself to join the others, all the others who resemble himself. "This man fears every kind of solitariness.... He is the man of the crowd. However small his stature, he takes every precaution to make it smaller, lest he stand out from the herd and find himself face to face with himself." He "attaches himself to a tradition and to a community—the tradition and community of the mediocre." He will do anything to escape from himself and from his freedom: "authentic liberty assumes responsibilities, and the liberty of the anti-Semite comes from the fact that he escapes all of his."[21]

The anti-Semite has favorite strategies for not coming to terms with himself. "He sees in the eyes of others a disquieting image—his own—and he makes his words and gestures conform to it. Having this external model, he is under no necessity to look for his personality within himself. He has chosen to be entirely outside himself, never to look within, to be nothing save the fear he inspires in others."[22] Equally dear to the anti-Semite is his claim to a history, so that he can hide in the past. Cherishing the memory of Vichy, each anti-Semite doubts not that he is a "true Frenchman, rooted in his province, in his country, borne along by a tradition twenty centuries old, benefiting from ancestral wisdom, guided by tried customs." The past is his, his possession, his identity, his right.[23] History, for the anti-Semite, is another route of escape from himself. He chooses to live outside the present because he is too cowardly to embrace the freedom that is an ontological given.

Constantly running away from himself, taking refuge in the crowd or in a mythological past, the anti-Semite would have no identity were it not for the Jews. Without the Jews, anti-Semites would be lost. "The anti-Semite is in the unhappy position of having a vital need for the very enemy he wishes to destroy." The supreme irony is that "if the Jew did not exist, the anti-Semite would have to invent him."[24]

It simply is not true, as is sometimes claimed, that Sartre's ethics of authenticity rules out nothing, since it most certainly condemns anti-Semitism and fascism. There is no such thing as an authentic fascist. All fascists are inauthentic and cannot be otherwise unless they stop being fascists and embrace the freedom they have shunned.[25]

*   *   *

The Jew is similar to the anti-Semite in that he yearns for a past. He has "a secret and deep-seated need to attach himself to tradition and, in default of a national past, to give oneself roots in a past of rites and customs." Yet

Jews "do not have the same fatherland; they have no history"; there is (in 1946) no Jewish state, so the Jewish people, judged by Hegelian standards, are not historical. "Its twenty centuries of dispersion and political impotence forbid its having a *historic past.* If it is true, as Hegel says, that a community is historical to the degree that it remembers its history, then the Jewish community is the least historical of all, for its keeps a memory of nothing but a long martyrdom." Even without Hegel, Sartre is willing to press his case: what the Jews have suffered, he argues, is "twenty centuries of repetition, not of evolution. The Jews are not yet *historical,* and yet they are the most ancient of peoples."[26]

The French title of Sartre's book is *Réflexions sur la Question Juive.* Rather than present this in English as *Reflections on the Jewish Question,* the translator took the liberty of rendering it *Anti-Semite and Jew.* It is difficult to fault the translator, given that his alternative title summarizes the thrust of Sartre's argument much better than the author's offering. Just as he had argued that the anti-Semite depends on the Jew he despises, so also does Sartre proclaim that "it is the anti-Semite who *makes* the Jew." "What unites Jews, even more than the sufferings of two thousand years, is the present hostility of Christians."[27]

Standing behind Sartre's claims that Jews have no history, nor an identity in their own right, are the pages in *Being and Nothingness* devoted to the "Other," "the Look"—the Sartrean reworking of Hegel's account of self and other. In Sartre's grand philosophical treatise, with the exception of a brief commentary on the bourgeoisie and the proletariat, his emphasis was on one-on-one relationships; in the essay of 1946, it is on the relationships not of individuals but of two groups, Jews and anti-Semites. The inescapable fate of the Jews is that they cannot but see themselves through the eyes, "the Look," of the anti-Semites. Their "common bond" is not a shared history but rather their "situation" of "living in a community which takes them for Jews."[28]

Probably the most objectionable pages in Sartre's pamphlet are those in which he enumerates "Jewish traits." While non-right-wing readers found what they wanted in his depiction of the anti-Semite, few could have welcomed his stereotypical treatment of the Jew. In summary fashion, he announced that Jews love money; lack tact; are overly ambitious; and often are uncomfortable in their own skins, afraid their bodies will give them away. These traits, he continued by way of justifying himself, had nothing to do with a (nonexistent) Jewish essence nor with a (nonexistent) Jewish history but were purely the result of the static Jewish situation. Ever defined as an outsider, as a member of a despised group, the Jew constantly favors what is universal, money for instance. For the same reasons, the Jew is contemptuous of whatever is particularistic; to him notions of "tact," for example, are based on an arbitrary social code, good for nothing except to enable some to feel superior to others. As for the ambition of Jews, it is a matter of wanting to gain entrance to exclusionary social circles.[29]

Of much greater interest is Sartre's discussion of authentic and inauthentic Jews. No sooner does he enter into this portion of his essay than many of his "Jewish traits" become more exactly understood as characteristics of the inauthentic Jew, the Jew who seeks to become "universal and anonymous." Living in denial, the inauthentic Jew "absorbs all knowledge with an avidity which is not to be confused with disinterested curiosity. He hopes to become … nothing but a man, a man like all other men, by taking in all the thoughts of man…. He cultivates himself in order to destroy the Jew in himself." A liberal, a humanist, an advocate of individual and human rights, he is no longer a Jew. Willingly he succumbs to the delusion that violence can be avoided: "the inauthentic Jew seeks to dissolve by critical analysis all that may separate men and lead them to violence."[30]

"Authenticity … is to live to the full his condition as Jew; inauthenticity is to deny it or to attempt to escape from it." The authentic Jew, he adds, is willing "to live in a situation that is defined precisely by the fact that it is unlivable." As imagined by Sartre, the authentic Jew is a super-existentialist: he is "this quintessence of man, disgraced, uprooted, destined from the start to either inauthenticity or martyrdom."[31] In his war diaries of 1940, Sartre had written that "it's much easier to live … authentically in wartime than in peacetime."[32] Six years later he appeared to suggest that Jews, in effect, always live in wartime, which is both their curse and their call to greatness.

In *Being and Nothingness,* it was Sartre's position that we are "condemned to be free," and that "we are not free to cease being free."[33] In the same work, he made use of Heidegger's expression that we have been "thrown" [*geworfen*] into the world and "thrown into a responsibility."[34] Here, again, in *Anti-Semite and Jew,* Sartre finds a new application for the familiar ontological rhetoric of his great philosophical treatise by affirming that "the Jew cannot choose not to be a Jew." Then, in a grand finale, he adds, "To be a Jew is to be thrown into—to be *abandoned to*—the situation of a Jew; and at the same time it is to be responsible in and through one's person for the destiny and the very nature of the Jewish people. For whatever the Jew says or does, … it is as if all his acts were subject to a Kantian imperative, as if he had to ask himself before each act: 'If all Jews acted as I am going to do, what would happen to Jewish life.'"[35]

In *Anti-Semite and Jew,* Sartre sketched a remarkable account of Jews by drawing upon his earlier notion of "self and other," complemented by his newer notion of "situation,"[36] but never did he immerse himself in the history of the Jews. Why, he seems to imply, should he write the history of a people who lived outside history?

The Unhistorical French Proletariat of the 1950s

Not everyone agreed, of course, with the proposition that Jews had lived and continue to live outside history, least of all Sartre's Jewish readers. Even Simone de Beauvoir would eventually complain that in *Anti-Semite and Jew* "the concrete factual basis necessary to a history of anti-Semitism is missing." In the postwar 1940s, she continued, Sartre "vacillated on history," as was evident in his treatment of the Jews.[37]

There are good reasons to agree with her. Many philosophical concepts from *Being and Nothingness* had found a home in Sartre's lean treatise on Jews and anti-Semites, but a historical sensibility was nowhere in evidence. Fear of freedom, attempts to escape by feigning an essence, conflict with the Other, bad faith, and inauthenticity were among the familiar philosophical elements. It was far from obvious, however, that Sartre, for all his references to France in recent times, had ever undertaken a serious study of French history or the place in it of anti-Semitism. There was a clear danger that Sartre's philosophy had dictated too many of his findings. Ontology, to all appearances, had trumped history.

Against the foregoing backdrop, the publication of *The Communists and Peace* may well be viewed as a stride forward in his intellectual development. Here, from 1952 to 1954, he could very readily have fallen into the same snare that had entrapped him several years earlier in *Anti-Semite and Jew.* Once again he set out to portray a group—the French proletariat of the 1950s—that had been beaten down so ferociously as to have lost its history. On this occasion, however, he offered a more satisfactory historical explanation of nonhistoricity.

Before it was a book, *The Communists and Peace* appeared as a series of essays in *Les Temps Modernes.* It was journalism, which is not the genre most conducive to a thoroughgoing historical treatment of a topic. Nor did the contemporaneous subject matter call out for a historical approach: his concern was the immediate one of why the workers had not heeded the Communist party's call to attend a vital rally, and why they likewise failed to comply with the party's request, a week later, that they hold a general strike. Seemingly everything conspired to tempt Sartre to ignore the past, as he had in *Anti-Semite and Jew.* And yet when he set forth another portrayal of humans forced to exist in a repetitive present, he outlined a historical explanation of how the workers had fallen, for the time being but not forever, outside history.

*   *   *

Sartre's insistence in *The Communists and Peace* that the French workers had been forced outside history has been overlooked in the scholarly literature. That, perhaps, is not surprising. Nowadays we all view Sartre's journalistic contributions in 1952 through the lens of Maurice Merleau-Ponty's attack on Sartre three years later in *Adventures of the Dialectic.* We are fascinated to observe Sartre placed on the defensive not by a party hack but a philosopher of his own stature. We find ourselves pondering whether it is true, as Merleau-Ponty suggested, that Sartre clung too closely to Cartesian dualism to develop a social theory and an accompanying historical outlook.

Were we, instead, to ask whether Sartre was once again on the prowl in *The Communists and Peace* for a group to join the Jews in the category of oppressed and ahistorical; were we to read his essays of the early 1950s while looking back to *Anti-Semite and Jew* rather than forward to *Adventures of the Dialectic,* we would encounter no difficulties in detecting Sartre's repeated claims that the workers had been temporarily removed from history.

In the early 1950s, wrote Sartre, "The French proletariat wonders if it has fallen outside of history." The workers of his day were "new men, without a tradition or a past." Whatever the history of the working class in France, whatever its past, its condition as observed by Sartre in his day was that "the masses do not have a collective memory and, since their 'awakenings' are intermittent, their action is always new, always begun over again without tradition."[38] If the workers have a history, they are unaware of it.

In an essay of 1945 dealing with the Occupation, Sartre had written that "a living person is above all a project.... But the Occupation stripped men of their future.... All our acts were merely provisional, their meaning limited to the day they were enacted."[39] Those same sentiments reappear in 1952, applied to the working class of France. "Today the future [of the workers] is blocked off." No longer does the worker have "the feeling of preparing the way" for the workers of the future. Once upon a time, "beyond the immediate objective, one saw the distant objective." No more: "he can still defend his interests, demand and obtain an increase in wages, but he establishes no relationship between this small, everyday victory and the destiny of the proletariat." For the worker there is no project; "he has lost his hold on history."[40]

Severed from the past, denied a future, "reduced to the immediate present, the worker no longer understands his history." Perhaps the bourgeoisie has a past and a future, but "the proletariat is crushed by a perpetual present." Repetition is the lot of the workers, mindless, mind-numbing repetition. "By fatigue and misery, by obliging him to reiterate the same gestures a thousand times a day, society discourages him from exercising his human qualities. He is enclosed in the insipid world of repetition; little by little he becomes a *thing.*"[41]

Much as Sartre had earlier composed a picture of Jews as the perpetual outsiders of French society, so did he later invite his readers to understand the proletarians as constituting "a society within society." The culture of which the French are so proud is not the worker's culture; "he couldn't care less." As for the freedom of which the French boast, what does it mean to a woman working in a refinery? "Her freedom doesn't resemble yours; ... she would gladly do without freedom ... if she were freed from the throbbing rhythm of the machines." The proletarians "participate in the economic life of the country but not in its social life." Sartre drives his argument to a climax: "One of the deepest and simplest feelings of the proletariat, one of the factors of his class consciousness, is this recognition of himself as pure *presence* [*être-là*] without any solidarity with the social whole. He is not integrated into society, he *lives alongside it,* in a semi-segregation."[42]

Still not finished, Sartre holds that history is for humans and therefore not for the workers because they are consistently treated as subhuman. The bourgeoisie is caught in a contradiction: its ideology of humanism dictates recognition of the dignity of the workers, "but the social order requires that the working class be kept in its bestial condition." On the job, the worker is constantly treated by the capitalist, in a reversal of Kantian ethics, as if he were merely a *thing,* a means, never an end.[43]

Time and again in *The Communists and Peace* we come into contact with the very same Sartre who wrote about the Resistance in "The Republic of Silence" and about Jews and anti-Semites two years afterward. Silence is still on his mind in 1952, if in a different sense: "I am writing this article in order to try to understand why France is silent."[44] The end of the war should have marked the end of silence, but the proletarians are still being silenced long after the so-called Liberation. "Refusal" was another of Sartre's favorite words when reflecting on the Resistance, and it, too, was reborn in the essays of 1952 where we read that the worker was engaged in "a tacit but constant refusal to be reduced to the state of a piece of machinery." The worker "*is* a subhuman when he simply accepts being what he is.… His human reality is not *in what he is* but *in his refusal to be such.*"[45] Finally, the word "martyrdom" is one Sartre applies to the workers, exactly as he had to the Jews.[46]

Beyond returning to the themes of "The Republic of Silence" and *Anti-Semite and Jew,* Sartre's essays on the French workers contain a number of asides in which he addressed contemporary politics through the grand vocabulary of philosophical existentialism. For example, at one point he remarked that the bourgeoisie has "shut the proletariat into a no-exit situation [*une situation sans issue*]." At another, he laments that "the worker feels *de trop,*" just as he had contended in *Nausea* and *Being and Nothingness* that we all feel superfluous, *de trop,* out of place. And how can Camus's *The Myth of Sisyphus* fail to come to mind when we read Sartre's remark that the worker "cannot have a presentiment of the sudden appearance of another universe and another *self* as the subject of history so long as he remains crushed on his rock?"[47]

It is difficult to deny that *The Communists and Peace* was written under the influence of Sartre's early works such as *Nausea* and *Being and Nothingness* in which history meant little or nothing. It is evident, moreover, that in *The Communists and Peace* he reprised his search in "The Republic of Silence" and *Anti-Semite and Jew* for a people denied a history. Nevertheless, despite the continuity of past themes, the writing of his essays on the proletarians represents a pivotal moment in Sartre's development; for in addition to the old themes, there is something new to which we must now turn, a deliberate effort to suggest a historical explanation of how a group became unhistorical.

* * *

Sartre aggressively charged the representatives of the French bourgeoisie with trying to "relieve" themselves of the need to "make a historical explanation" of the relationship between workers and bourgeoisie. Their talk about the "proletariat-in-itself" and "capitalism-in-itself" aimed to avoid an understanding of the historical proletariat. By contrast, he attempted to offer the very historical account that is lacking in the thought of the apologists of the established order. "The French proletariat is a historical reality whose singularity was made manifest in recent years," argued Sartre. "I do not go looking for the key to its attitude in the universal movement of societies, but in the movement of French society; that is to say, in the history of France." The abstract must yield to the concrete: "Leaving eternal France at grips with the proletariat-in-itself, I am undertaking to explain events rigorously defined in time and space by the peculiar structure of our economy, and the latter in turn by certain events of our local history."[48]

It is quite true that "the workers have disappeared from official history"; how could it be otherwise, Sartre asked, given that the bourgeoisie has striven to remove them mentally from the past, much as it has physically forced the poor "outside the walls" of Paris—out of sight and out of mind. By no means, however, has the bourgeoisie been entirely successful in its efforts to obliterate the past. There is "a proletariat forged by a hundred and fifty years of struggle" and on occasion it is still "conscious of its traditions and grandeur."[49]

Alas, by and large, that was the proletariat that was—the proletariat of yesteryear. In the 1950s, as opposed to former ages, "the heroic times of anarcho-syndicalism" are no more, mechanization has made machines of men, revolutionary aspirations are on the wane, the masses have replaced the classes, and "the heroic and bloody history of the proletariat" is past and forgotten.[50] The mechanization of work "alters human relationships," turning what once were classes into modern day "masses." Within factories, the most outstanding product of machines is not physical objects but these nonhuman human beings, "the masses."[51]

At the time Sartre wrote the foregoing words, nothing was more common within the English-speaking world than for intellectuals such as Hannah Arendt, viewing society from the top down, to sound the alarm that the degeneration of class society into "mass society" threatened to open the door to revolutionary movements.[52] Sartre, taking a bottom-up perspective, stipulated precisely the contrary proposition: the advent of the masses meant that the workers had lost their commitment to revolution.

The proletariat of 1900, according to Sartre, was "profoundly differentiated," unlike that of his own time, which was "amorphous and homogeneous." In the 1950s, the proletarians are "alone together," their solidarity shattered. "Let us not conclude, however, that this isolation is *natural.* ... No, the isolation of the worker doesn't come from nature; it is *produced*"—by the bourgeoisie in the setting of the factory.[53]

The growth of the unskilled working force and the decline of skilled artisans has ground the forward historical movement of the proletariat to a halt. The unskilled or semiskilled worker does not know where he belongs in "a society devoid of institutions to protect him or words to name the wrong being done to him." "Half accomplice, half victim, participant and martyr," he is "simultaneously a man and a piece of machinery." Around the turn of the century, the Syndicalist movement still thrived, Fernand Pelloutier preached his *ouvriérisme,* and master craftsmen took pride in their work. Later in the century, "the skilled worker had had his day. Meanwhile, the semiskilled workers multiplied and unionism vegetated ... ; to these new men, without a tradition or a past, the old militants no longer had anything to say."[54]

In sum, Sartre's historical account of the nonhistorical proletariat of his day amounts to this: the modernization of France and the "rationalization" of industry profoundly altered the composition of the working class. As the ranks of the unskilled workers swelled, the structures of the proletariat were "liquidated," and the newly formed "masses" were "removed from the influence of the workers' 'elite.'"[55] The proletarians were adrift, leaderless, and condemned to watch history pass them by.

*   *   *

This process of rationalization of industry, in Sartre's view, was one the bourgeoisie in France, unlike that in England or America, had only halfway adopted. Supposedly the advocates of economic innovation, in truth the French bourgeois feared the consequences of widespread change and made it their business to hold the economy in check. "We must stop history,"[56] was their whispered creed. Their self-conscious intention was to minimize economic change, the better to negate social and political change.[57]

The reign of scarcity, of "Malthusianism,"[58] wrote Sartre in *The Communists and Peace,* has been imposed by the French capitalists on their countrymen. To that end, the bourgeoisie had chosen to suppress ardent competitiveness by "preserving the archaic dispersion of our stores and factories." The point of this refusal to modernize, this unwillingness to claim the advantages of economies of scale or to expand markets, was to infect the minds of the workers with the thought that betterment of their lot was impossible.[59]

While the bourgeois want profits, they are far more concerned with protecting the social status of their families and holding the workers in check. "Does the number of strikes increase with production? Then the bourgeois will prevent production from increasing. If it falls below a certain level, are insurrectional disturbances to be feared? Then they will make sure that production doesn't decrease either." Stagnant wages and despair of improving one's social standing are the consequence of low productivity, which is "the constitutional vice of our economy."[60] French society and the workers mired in its immobility move neither forward nor back, toward neither the past nor the future.

Sartre's argument is all the more noteworthy if we take into consideration that in 1963 two prominent scholars, Michel Crozier in France and Stanley Hoffmann in America, published works discussing France in the 1950s and earlier as a "stalemate" or "stalled" society.[61] Both men were liberals; neither had a Sartrean bone in his body, nor did either share Sartre's sympathy for the French Communist party. Yet their depiction of France as an immobile society bears at least a family resemblance to Sartre's presentation in *The Communists and Peace* and inadvertently casts a friendly light on Sartre's argument.

On his side, Sartre, if given the chance, might have uttered a few kind words about the efforts of Crozier and Hoffmann, especially if he were to take into account their links with *Les Temps Modernes.* Crozier wrote articles for that journal at the same time Sartre was writing his on the French workers, and Hoffmann was the student of one of the original editors of the magazine, Raymond Aron. Tocqueville, not Marx, was their hero, but even that would not necessarily have put off Sartre, who admired Tocqueville's historical writings, especially his thoughts on the revolution of 1848, as much as he hated those of other liberal intellectuals.[62]

Speaking as devoted liberals rather than revolutionaries, Crozier and Hoffmann unconsciously echoed Sartre's words describing an immobile France. Not the maximization of productivity but the maintenance of the family firm was the primary objective of the bourgeoisie, they affirmed. Because of a history of political instability, the French craved social stability above all else, sacrificing economic progress if necessary. The French, distrustful of one another; identifying with a group or class only to gain protection from other groups or classes; shunning face-to-face relationships, hiding behind abstract, impersonal rules, did their utmost to slow down the clock of history.

Obviously Sartre would have disagreed vehemently with the contention of Crozier and Hoffmann that uprisings in the streets were largely ritualistic undertakings aimed at forcing the State to settle the grievances that capital and labor could not resolve on their own. He might, however, have taken deep satisfaction at the thought that two liberals had done so much to vindicate the views about history he espoused a decade earlier. His view of France in general and its proletariat in particular as standing outside history was coincidentally but significantly reinforced by Crozier and Hoffmann.

In *Anti-Semite and Jew* Sartre's argument for placing the Jews outside history was unconvincing, formulaic, and smacked of trying to force the data into the pre-established categories of Sartrean ontology. By contrast, *The Communists and Peace* featured a much more historical argument, confirmed by ideological adversaries, that a group could be and had been removed from history. It is a measure of how far Sartre had advanced that much of what he said about the French workers in 1952 would reappear in the historically sophisticated *Critique of Dialectical Reason.*[63]

The History of Non-Historicity in the Third World

Sartre's next candidates for those called upon either to capitulate to their forcible removal from history or to fight back, against all odds, were the peoples who from the early 1950s onward were placed by French intellectuals under the rubric of the "Third World."[64] More perhaps than any other European country, the domestic politics of France was dominated by the international problems of the period, especially the question of decolonization. Whether he was writing about Algeria, the Congo, or pre-Castro Cuba, about China or Vietnam, Sartre in the 1950s and 1960s viewed the world through the eyes of "the wretched of the earth," much as he had previously viewed the politics of France in *The Communists and Peace* through "the eyes of the least favored."[65]

Although Sartre's introduction to Frantz Fanon's *The Wretched [les Damnés] of the Earth* (1961) is the most frequently cited of his writings on the "Third World," many of its arguments may be found both in his earlier and his later writings. One of his constant themes was that the culture of colonized peoples had been destroyed and their history stolen. In an essay of 1956, he charged that the French colonists were out "to destroy the internal structures of Algerian society." In "Frenchifying and dividing up the property, the structure of the old tribal society was broken up without putting anything in its place." Sartre had no doubt that "a necessary aspect of the colonial system is that it attempts to bar the colonized people from the road of history," and what better way to cut the Muslims off from their past than to deny them, as the French colonizers had, the use of their own language?[66]

Much later, commenting on Vietnam in 1967, Sartre wrote that "colonization is not a matter of mere conquest.... It is, of necessity, cultural genocide.... The colonized peoples lose their national individuality, their culture, and their customs." Likewise, "social structures are destroyed.... Family life—so deeply respected by the Vietnamese—no longer exists.... Every possibility of religious or cultural life has been suppressed."[67] Along the same lines, in the most formal of his reflections on history, the *Critique of Dialectical Reason*, we read that "in a colonized country, the pauperization of the masses destroyed the structures of the old society, and removed the means of reconstituting another, based on different structures and on different relations of sociality."[68] One of the constants in Sartre's reflections on the consequences of colonization was that the ties between the natives and their past have been severed completely, and there is no point in trying to recover lost roots.

The oft–commented-on introduction to Fanon makes the same point and then adds another dimension to the foregoing comments. In keeping with his reflections elsewhere, Sartre writes that "Everything will be done to wipe out the traditions of the natives, to substitute our language for theirs and to destroy their culture without giving them ours." But then he strikes a different note, a demand that the wretched of the earth seize the future by rising up in revolution: "The reader [of Fanon] is sternly put on his guard against.... Western culture, and what is equally to be feared, the withdrawal into the twilight of past African culture. For the only true culture is that of the revolution; that is to say, it is constantly in the making."[69] Something good, something desirable can come from cultural annihilation and deprivation. With their past destroyed and no present in which to live, Third World peoples may feel compelled to lay claim to the future.

There are other respects in which Sartre's famous and infamous introduction to Fanon both builds on and surpasses his earlier writings. To begin with the continuities, in *The Communists and Peace* he remarks that the proletarian is subhuman, "neither man nor beast,"[70] living proof that no matter how loudly the bourgeoisie touts "humanism" in theory, its practice is such as to "blow humanism apart." Throughout the text of his essays on the French proletariat in 1952, there recurs the motif of humanism proclaimed by the upper class but denied to the under class.[71] These themes of the reduction of human beings to animals, to subhumans, and of the perversion of humanist doctrines into pillars supporting inhumane treatment of the downtrodden recur in Sartre's writings of the 1950s on colonialism and imperialism and culminate in his preface to Fanon.

In 1957, Sartre charged that "colonialism denies *human rights* to people it has subjugated by violence." Faced with its Declaration of Human Rights, "the colonist can absolve himself only by systematically pursuing the 'dehumanization' of the colonized." The colonial exploiters choose to regard the natives as "subhuman," as "animals that talk."[72] The previous year, he had applied the same analysis to the case of Algeria: "since all human beings have the same rights, the Algerian will be made a subhuman."[73] So we have every reason to be prepared for Sartre's assertion in 1961, in his introduction to Fanon, that the French are guilty of hypocrisy and that although our "humanism claims that we are at one with the rest of humanity, our racist methods set us apart." We enlightened Frenchmen, "so liberal and humane," we the authors of the Declaration of Human Rights, "pretend to forget that we own colonies and that in them men are massacred."

Sartre insists in his gloss to Fanon on underscoring the manner in which the colonists attempt to reduce the colonized to a subhuman status but are prevented by their material interests from completing their despicable program. "When you domesticate a member of your own species, you reduce his output.... For this reason the settlers are obliged to stop the breaking-in halfway; the result, neither man nor animal, is the native." Between the French proletarian of 1952 and the native, there is a profound similarity: both have been denied their humanity.

There is also a considerable difference. Sartre's proletarian of 1952, incapable of acting on his own, is "a 'subhuman' who joins the party in order to become a man." By way of significant contrast, Sartre's native of 1961 is a subhuman who takes his fate into his own hands, no matter whether a Communist party is waiting to organize him. The natives "have become men: men *because* of the settler, who wants to make beasts of burden of them—because of him, and against him. Hatred, blind hatred ... is their only wealth; the Master calls it forth because he seeks to reduce them to animals, but he fails to break it down because his interests stop him halfway."[74]

More than ever before, Sartre demanded in his treatment of colonized peoples that the victims of oppression force their way, on their own initiative and on their own terms, into history. Resistance and refusal were now only the beginning; the time had come for the Third World to make history. Clearly, new developments had entered into Sartre's long-standing discussion of non-historical peoples. He found himself in full agreement with Fanon's statement that "It is a question of the Third World starting a new history of Man."[75]

Old Thoughts and New

Both the old and the new in Sartre's thought stood out in bold relief in his introduction to Fanon. As in the past, he continued to write about "resistance," about "refusal" and saying "no": "we only become what we are by the radical and deep-seated negation of that which others have made of us"; that is, by "a stubborn refusal of the animal condition." The theme of holding out while suffering torture—a favorite from the times of the Resistance—likewise recurred when he addressed what the French authorities were doing to beat down the activist natives. And if in *The Flies,* his play on the Resistance, he wrote that "human life begins on the far side of despair,"[76] then in his introduction to Fanon, he wrote "we find our humanity on this side of death and despair; the native finds his beyond torture and death."[77]

Finally, there is continuity in his comments on "the Look." Surely a parallel exists between his insistence that the Jew was defined by the look of the other and his similar insistence that the look of the settler torments the native. As early as 1948, Sartre had written, "For three thousand years the white man has enjoyed the privilege of seeing without being seen; he was pure look."[78] Come the year 1961, he again stressed how the "Other," the settler, by means of his "look" locked the native into a dreadful situation of "self" and "other" in which the settler was cast as "Master" and the native as "Slave."

What is new in the introduction to Fanon is the completion of the dialectic of Master and Slave that was halted in midcourse in *Anti-Semite and Jew.* In both 1946 and 1961, Sartre implicitly drew on Alexandre Kojève's famous lectures delivered in the 1930s, published as a book under the title *Introduction to the Reading of Hegel.*[79] Kojève placed the struggle between master and slave at the heart of human history, no matter that in the *Phenomenology of Mind* the discussion of the transition from consciousness to self-consciousness, and the accompanying commentary on master and slave, takes place before Hegel has turned to his account of the march of Spirit through the ages. In a kind of deliberate Marxian misreading and reworking of Hegel, Kojève has the slave winning out against the master throughout the course of the centuries.[80] No passage in the *Phenomenology* is more useful in this imposition of Marx on Hegel than the one dealing with labor: "precisely in labor," wrote Hegel, "where there seemed to be merely some outsider's mind and ideas involved, the slave becomes aware, through this re-discovery of himself by himself, of having and being a 'mind of his own.'"[81]

For Sartre, as for many other French intellectuals of his generation, Kojève's creative misreading of Hegel was one he valued because it could be adapted to his own purposes. As we previously noted, Sartre made political use of the master/slave dichotomy as early as "The Republic of Silence" in 1944. There, he sided with the slave as contrasted with Nietzsche who had sided with the master. Nowhere, however, in Sartre's writings immediately following the war did he show much interest in the completion of a "dialectical" development, which would be for the slave to rise up and replace the master. "Authenticity" was Sartre's focus, and it was much more likely to be found in the ranks of slaves than masters. Initially, then, Sartre was drawn to the categories of Kojève's Hegel but on his own terms; completing the dialectical movement was not on his agenda. Sartre remained mired in the viewpoint expressed in *Being and Nothingness* where he had written, "there is no dialectic for my relations toward the Other but rather a circle.... We can never get outside the circle."[82]

By the time he responded to Fanon, the focus of Sartre's work had changed substantially. He still sided with the slaves but would not stop until they had become masters, in control of their circumstances, traveling along a road they had paved from present to future. Simone de Beauvoir was correct to suggest that Fanon had been deeply influenced by Sartre's *Critique of Dialectical Reason*[83]; but we must add what she omitted, that Sartre was influenced by Fanon. It was Fanon who helped spur Sartre to complete the dialectical movement and to do so by placing "violence" rather than "labor" at the center of the phenomenology of Master and Slave.

Fanon's *The Wretched of the Earth* has been called the manifesto of Third World revolution; it might also be called "in praise of violence" and was appreciated as such by Sartre. Drawing on his training as a psychologist, Fanon added a new dimension to the familiar argument that the colonizers inflict egregious harm on the colonized. It is not only the bodies of the natives that suffer at the hands of the settlers; so do their minds, their psyches. In an earlier book, *Black Skins, White Masks* (1952), Fanon had shown how deeply colonized peoples had been wounded by their oppressors. Racism scars its victims physically, of course, but perhaps inflicts even more harm psychologically. Fanon's contention was that racism is internalized by its very victims, a finding later seconded by psychiatrists in other countries, including America. Robert Coles, in a study of the first black students to integrate schools in the American South, found that they drew pictures of whites as fully developed but of blacks as lacking one or another limb and with faces only partially colored.[84]

When he wrote *The Wretched of the Earth*, Fanon posited a "regular and constant mental pathology" that was "the direct product of oppression." The native's affliction was a colonial neurosis and the therapy was violence, even "absolute violence." "The violence which has ruled over the ordering of the colonial world ... will be claimed and taken over by the native." Violence "frees the native from his inferiority complex and from his despair and inaction; it makes him fearless and restores his self-respect." Mischievously, Fanon steals the old conservative metaphor of social classes as a hierarchical "great chain of being," transfiguring it into a great chain of violence: "The practice of violence binds [the natives] together as a whole, since each individual forms a violent link in the great chain, a part of the great organism of violence."[85]

Sartre did not hesitate to build on Fanon's eulogy of violence. He portrayed the Third World revolutionaries not as brothers who kill because they must but as men who become brothers when they kill, "and may at any moment have to kill again." Violence, he wrote provocatively, is humanism: "the child of violence, at every moment the native draws from it his humanity." It is also the highest creativity, that of "man re-creating himself." In common with Fanon, he wrote that "the same violence is thrown back upon us as when our reflection comes forward to meet us when we go toward a mirror." Also in agreement with Fanon, he added, "The native cures himself of colonial neurosis by thrusting out the settler through force of arms."[86]

Seemingly Sartre's argument is cribbed in every respect from *The Wretched of the Earth*. We must not, however, fail to recognize something quite his own rather than a gloss of Fanon. Deeply embedded in Sartre's essay, but not in Fanon's book,[87] is the language of Master and Slave. This is not the first time one encounters it in Sartre's work, but it is essential to take notice that he has moved well beyond his previous position of admiring the slave, praising the slave's willingness to endure torture and to sacrifice himself to the larger cause. Rather than confine himself to commending those who were willing to face up to the present intolerable situation—"authentic" Jews, for example—he is now hailing those who want to move into the future. The dialectic can be completed if, but only if, the slave supplants the master and through revolutionary violence takes the future into his own hands.

It would be a fatal mistake to think that Sartre's response to Fanon was an anomaly in his writings. Perhaps the extreme and untroubled praise of violence stands alone, but the mixture of old themes with the new one of seizing history and marching into the future was repeated on other occasions. At almost the same time that he was dealing with Algeria and *The Wretched of the Earth*, we find him visiting Cuba and commenting on that country. Again, there is the old rhetoric of "torture and death," of "refusal," of a "broken, atomized society," of a "disinherited class," of Cuban people for whom the past was gone and who, "up until 1959, had no future. They lived for the moment." But in his journalism on Cuba, as in his thoughts on

Fanon or his reflections in the *Critique of Dialectical Reason,* he no longer settled for resistance. Only revolution will do, which entails saying farewell to past and present in a quest for the invention of a novel and beckoning future. In Cuba, thanks to the Revolution, "men make History."[88]

*   *   *

Around 1960 or even a few years earlier, Sartre's attention turned more toward the Third World, less toward the Western proletariat. More and more, he wanted revolution and the future, not resistance and the present. By 1960, he was worried, as were other radical intellectuals in Europe and America, that the workers may have been successfully bought off by a capitalism that was advancing in France as elsewhere, no matter how long the French economy of the past had lagged behind Germany, England, and America. The successes of the welfare state did not bode well for revolution.

In any case, gaining the support of the French workers for revolutionary movements in the Third World, no matter what the situation of the French economy, had never been an easy task. By his own admission, the proletariat of 1952 could act only when acted on by the Communist party, a great obstacle because Sartre was ever denouncing the party's foot-dragging policies on Algeria. Beyond the party, the workers themselves were the problem, as he realized as early as 1948, when writing about black and Madagascan poets in "Black Orpheus." At best, white workers in France and blacks in the Third World have little in common; at worst "the white worker, in spite of himself, benefits marginally from colonization: however low his standard of living, it would be even lower without it."[89]

At the beginning of "Black Orpheus," he spoke as he had two years earlier when the topic was the supposedly timeless Jews. Authenticity was his initial theme: "The Negro cannot deny that he is a Negro, nor lay claim to an abstract colorless humanity: he is black. Hence he is backed forcibly into authenticity." But later in "Black Orpheus" he offered us what in retrospect is a preview of his subsequent insistence, especially in 1960 and 1961, that resistance is not enough; saying "no" must be complemented by revolution, that is, by an insistence upon entering the flow of history. Through suffering, he insisted in 1948, "black consciousness becomes historical"; "race has been transmuted into historicity, the black Present explodes and temporalizes itself"; the black man "historicizes himself insofar as suffering confers upon him a collective past and assigns him a goal in the future."[90]

When Sartre turned his attention to the Third World he resolved a fundamental tension in his thought, dating back to two brief essays he wrote in the mid-1940s. Emerging from the war he published "Occupied Paris," in which he complained that France had been forcibly removed from history for four years, and expressed deep satisfaction that "our fate is [now] in our hands"—the future was open for the French to construct.[91] On the other hand, there was the Sartre of the very same time who in "The Republic of Silence" seemed to envy the years when men and women had no future and could not retreat to the past but were forced either to be authentic or cowards. A frozen present with no recourse to the past or future was much to Sartre's liking.

Which would Sartre choose: a continuation of the quest for the unhistorical that was his in *Anti-Semite and Jew* and still his as late as 1952 through 1954 in *The Communists and Peace,* or history understood as the construction of the future? His encounters with the Third World were exceptionally useful in deciding the issue. After his initiation into the struggles taking place outside the frontiers of Europe, all his efforts would be devoted to the support of those who were preoccupied with seizing the world, plunging into history, forging the future in defiance of Europe. Resistance should continue but its proper place would henceforth be within the framework of Revolution.

Reinterpreting Freedom

When Sartre moved beyond "resistance" occurring outside the stream of history to "revolution" within its flow, he found himself altering his initial position on freedom. Many scholars have exercised considerable analytical rigor in efforts to demonstrate in depth that Sartre's understanding of freedom later in his career was not what it was at the beginning. It is not our concern to enter into all of those debates, but only to make the point that his changing attitude toward politics and history dictated that he drop the concept of freedom floating in the background of such early writings as "The Republic of Silence" and *Anti-Semite and Jew.* He could not permit his bold program for the Third World to be undermined by conceptual residues dating back to *Being and Nothingness.*

The old notion of a group denied its history frequently reasserted itself when he wrote about Algeria, Cuba, or other countries of the Third World. But no longer did Sartre have room for the Stoic view of freedom which, be it recalled, permeated "The Republic of Silence" and *Anti-Semite and Jew.* As early as 1947, Sartre indicated he had changed his mind. The oppressed, he wrote in *What is Literature?,* "hide from themselves their complicity with the oppressors when they claim that one can remain free in chains if one has a taste for the inner life."[92] Repeatedly in his notebooks of 1947 to 1948, Sartre sustained his breakthrough rejection of Stoic freedom and warned that Stoic ideas encourage collusion with the enemy.[93]

Later, as in the *Critique of Dialectical Reason*,[94] he explicitly continued to repudiate his original views about freedom in chains. When Simone de Beauvoir and Sartre sat down for a dialogue in 1974, she questioned him directly on the issue of his changing notion of freedom. "Basically," said de Beauvoir to Sartre, "your conception of freedom was that of the Stoic—that which does not depend on us has no importance and that which does depend on us is freedom. One is therefore free in any situation, any circumstances." As their conversation progressed, Sartre explicitly agreed with her assessment of his early work: "*Being and Nothingness* is a book about freedom. I then, like the old Stoics, believed that one was always free, even in exceedingly disagreeable circumstances that might end in death," but, he was careful to add, "on this point I've changed very much."

Why he had changed was also pointed out by de Beauvoir. Within his now discarded mental universe, in her words, "there's no longer any need to do anything.... One can confine oneself to one's own inner life." Politically speaking, the adoption of such Stoic (and Cartesian) views could lead to "extremely reactionary attitudes." Sartre agreed and then, at her urging, named the moment of recognition when he had been jolted out of his previous views: it was his discovery that he was not only a temporal but also a historical being. "My idea of freedom has been modified by my relations with history. I was within history; whether I liked it or not I was carried along in the direction of certain social changes."[95]

Captivity, Occupation, Resistance—all these, by his own account, had plunged him into history during and immediately following World War II. Once inside history, he had no choice but to stay. Inevitably, as he identified more and more oppressed groups and militated for their freedom, he came to see freedom as a goal to be pursued, an arduous collective task rather than a given. "In order to make my freedom triumph it was necessary to act upon history and the world and bring about a different relation between man on the one hand and history and the world on the other."[96]

Postscript: Simone de Beauvoir on the Non-History of Women

In her famous book *The Second Sex,* published in 1948, Simone de Beauvoir set out to save women from their historical exile and to save her companion, Sartre, from himself. While her method of reasoning in discussing women is reminiscent of Sartre's earlier and later works that dealt with groups he deemed nonhistorical, her argument could only proceed by a prior expurgation of his comments on women in his philosophical works.

Whatever the glories of *Being and Nothingness,* Sartre's willingness to turn ontology into an excuse for misogyny cannot be counted among their number. Being-in-itself, as presented in 1943, is sticky, soft, syrupy, wet—reason enough for Garcin to repel Estelle's advances in *No Exit* by saying, "You're soft and slimy, ... like an octopus, like a quagmire."[97] Consciousness, Being-for-itself, creates an opening, a hole, in the fullness of being—reason enough to speak of women as holes in being: "The obscenity of the feminine sex," he wrote in *Being and Nothingness,* "is that of everything which 'gapes open.'" A page later: "her sex is a mouth which devours the penis—a fact which can easily lead to the idea of castration. The amorous act is the castration of the man; but this is above all because sex is a hole."[98] And what could be more nauseating than Roquentin's account in *Nausea* of his sexual encounter with a woman?[99] Quite possibly, there is only one direct, substantive agreement between Sartre and de Beauvoir on women around 1948, the statement in his notebooks—which she would put to good use—that woman was "the Other in History."[100]

Late in Sartre's life, in 1974, de Beauvoir extracted from him the straightforward statement "I do think that men and women are equal."[101] She was also quite adept at undermining, in 1983, his original Stoical notions by asking "What is the freedom of women in a harem?"[102] What truly mattered, however, was her remarkable intellectual performance many years earlier when she published *The Second Sex.* Within the pages of this, perhaps her most influential book, she arguably made a more compelling case for a group that had been denied a history than anything Sartre offered before or after 1948 when he expounded the same theme. In her view, Jews, blacks, and other persons who figured prominently on Sartre's list of non-historical peoples, do in fact have a history. "The Jewish diaspora, the introduction of slavery in America, the colonial conquests ...—for the oppressed in these cases there was a *before*: they had a past in common, a tradition, sometimes a religion, a culture."[103] It is women, and perhaps women alone, who fit well into Sartre's specifications for a group denied a history through the centuries.

Thanks to existentialism, de Beauvoir could quickly dispose of the notion that a woman's ahistorical "nature" or "essence" was what defined her. "In the human collectivity nothing is natural," everything is cultural and acquired. "To explain her limits, it is her situation that one must invoke and not a mysterious essence." The way to arrive at an understanding of woman's situation was to provide an account of her history, even if she has been denied the kind of history known to men.[104]

Repetition, "monotonous repetition," is the lot that has ever been imposed on women. "Time has for her no dimension of novelty, is not a bursting forward; because she is devoted to repetition, she sees in the future only a repetition of the past." Her daily tasks of cooking and motherhood never change. Man "envisages history as a becoming," whereas woman, denied a "project," is "suspicious of the future and wishes to stop time." Change she comes to view as a threat, so it is not surprising that women opposed the labor movement in the nineteenth century or that Southern women in America passionately supported slavery. How could it be otherwise, given that from the Greeks to contemporary times "her condition has remained the same."[105]

Locked in a prison of jewelry and flowers when she is upper class, and sheer drudgery when she is lower class, woman wishes to *have* because she cannot *do*; she cannot act. She cannot attain the most elevated attitudes, those of "heroism, revolt, detachment, invention, creation."[106] Nor does she have at her disposal the means of collective action available to others: women lack "the concrete means of organizing themselves into a unity.... They have no past, no history, no religion of their own; and have not, like the proletarians, a solidarity of work and interests." "Other" in the world of man, she is on the outside looking in but imagines she is on the inside looking out. "Proletarians say 'we'; blacks also. Taking themselves for subjects, they change the bourgeois and whites into 'others.' Women, however, ... do not say 'we.'" They do not recognize they are oppressed or at least fail to realize that they are oppressed in common.[107]

Unlike the Jews portrayed by Sartre in 1946, Simone de Beauvoir's women of 1948 are no longer imprisoned in a present that is nothing more than an endless repetition of the past. For de Beauvoir, there is no reason why women cannot enter history in the modern world. "Open her future and she will no longer cling to the past.... Open her future and she will no longer be obliged to settle down in the present." De Beauvoir finishes with a tone of hope one rarely finds in Sartre: "it seems virtually certain that women will arrive, sooner or later, at a perfect economic and social equality which will initiate an internal metamorphosis."[108]

Simone de Beauvoir may have borrowed Sartre's thoughts on the historical search for the unhistorical, but she made them her own and quite possibly surpassed him in this realm. She knew when to claim that a group had been denied a history, when not. Fears that a group granted a past might become inauthentic did not prevent her from exploring the future possibilities of women. And, unlike Sartre, she did not insist on revolution as the only path to the future. Feminists could win, eventually, without resorting to the politics of violence. Her two volumes on the trek of women throughout history fulfilled Sartre's program and projected his way of thinking beyond his horizons.

Chapter 4

Human History and the Human Condition

No matter how far Sartre advanced down the road of historical thinking, it remains true that residues of his previous ahistorical or non-historical philosophizing lingered problematically in his writings. His forward intellectual trajectory toward full immersion in the study of history may be characterized in various ways, but no one is entitled to say it was linear, smooth, or unbroken. The "eddies" and "discontinuous zigzags," the "contradictory whirling of history" that he remarked on as recurring phenomena *in history* were possibly even more evident in his reflections *on history*.[1]

Of all the complications that bedeviled his efforts, perhaps none was more marked than the tension in his thought between invocations of the "human condition" and examinations of human history. Sartre wanted to have both at his disposal, to yield neither: he wished to continue adhering to the venerable philosophical notion of the "human condition" at the same time that he embraced new fangled historicism. But these two are an uneasy match: the human condition normally pertaining to what is universal, fixed, and timeless, whereas human history is particular, changing, and time-bound.

In 1946, he wrote, "although it is impossible to find in each and every man a universal essence that can be called human nature, there is nevertheless a human universality of *condition*."[2] Addressing his readers a year later, he sounded a different note, remarking that an author should write "not about the abstract man of all the ages and for a timeless reader, but about the whole man of his age and for his contemporaries."[3] Anyone who looks carefully at Sartre's publications in 1946 and 1947 is bound to notice that during these two years he spoke constantly about both the "human condition" and the need for writers "to produce a literature of historicity."[4] What, then, was the relationship between discussions of human history and the "human condition?" Could Sartre somehow forge ahead with the study of history and yet continue contributing to the centuries-old conversation about the "human condition?"

Even if the notion of the "human condition" threatened to compromise Sartre's budding efforts to assume the mantle of historian, he could not readily abandon his trans-historical philosophical quest. Rebel though he was born to be, he nevertheless tipped his hat, in his fashion, to a discourse that had prospered for ages in French intellectual circles. From Montaigne to his own time, reflections on the "human condition" had been central to the proud culture of his country. Pascal, who set forth one of the most memorable conceptions of the "human condition," was in particular some-one whom Sartre could not mention too often, at least in passing, from his early writings to his finale, *The Family Idiot*. And then there was André Malraux, whose novel *La Condition Humaine*, translated into English under the questionable title *Man's Fate*, Sartre commented on repeatedly in his writings. Why the translator did not choose *The Human Condition* is un-clear, but the failure to do so surely underscores how the English-speaking world sometimes fails to understand things French. Presumably, the last thing one should do is to remove Malraux's famous book of 1933 from the grand French dialogue over the "human condition."

Malraux's book predates Sartre's career by several years. In Sartre's own time as a mature and influential figure, Albert Camus published two books on the human condition, both frequently cited and praised by Sartre, *The Myth of Sisyphus* and *The Plague*. Finally, there was Samuel Beckett, who in *Waiting for Godot* brilliantly proved that the stage could be used to dramatize the human condition, and not just any version of the human condition but that of Jean-Paul Sartre, as enunciated in *Being and Nothingness*.

Astonishing as Beckett's play was, perfect as was its dramatization of Sartre's philosophy, it did not solve Sartre's problem. Yes, it powerfully sec-onded Sartre's argument in *Being and Nothingness* that the experience of time should be considered as a central aspect of the human condition, but it added nothing at all to Sartre's few comments on history in his philosophical treatise, history having nothing to do with Beckett's play. The question of the relationship between history and a seemingly trans-historical human condition remained as pressing after the final curtain as it had before the audience was seated.

There were moments when the story of the place of the "human condition" in Sartre's ever more historically oriented thought seemed all but settled, in favor of history. Following his thought chronologically, one may be tempted to draw the conclusion that the "human condition" progressively disappeared from his discourse, yielding pride of place to historical preoccupations: out with the old, in with the new. Again, it might well be suggested that the "human condition" yielded more and more to Sartre's political commitments that are as specific, here and now, as the "human condition" is abstract and elsewhere. Yet it would be quite wrong to infer that the "human condition" eventually faded out of Sartre's thought. Always it was there, just under the surface when not out in the open, sometimes more marginalized, sometimes less; and time and again, after seemingly having been driven out of his thought by his newer preoccupations with history and politics, it succeeded in staging a comeback.

Strikingly, not even Camus's *The Rebel* was enough to eliminate allusions to the "human condition" in Sartre's final writings. If ever Sartre had been likely to make the final break, the publication of Camus's book in 1951 would presumably have been the moment. For *The Rebel* incurred the lasting wrath of the *Les Temps Modernes* group because Camus championed the "human condition" for the purpose of condemning historicism and revolutionary politics. Inevitably, Sartre and his cohort spoke thereafter as if discussions of the "human condition" were hopelessly old fashioned, outmoded, and reactionary.

Nevertheless, the term "human condition" surreptitiously reappeared in Sartre's writings after he and his partisans had finished blasting Camus. The tale of how the notion of the "human condition" functions in Sartre's thought does not end in a decisive final chapter wherein the loose ends are tied up, the riddles solved. But that is no reason to fret: the richness of the story lies in its very ambiguity. We should not resolve what Sartre left unresolved; rather, our task is to bear witness to the fascinating tensions in his reflections.

Two Visions of the "Human Condition"

The starting point of our analysis of the relationship between the "human condition" and history in Sartre's thought must be a discussion of his early thoughts on *la condition humaine*. At once, however, we encounter the difficulty that not one but two accounts figure in his early works: The first hails from books written before and during the war, *Nausea* and *Being and Nothingness,* and achieves a perfect fulfillment in Beckett's *Waiting for Godot.* The second version has its *locus classicus* in Sartre's publications during the years immediately following the war, *Anti-Semite and Jew* for one, *What Is Literature?* for another.

It does not suffice, however, to observe that Sartre offered two versions of the "human condition." What must be added is that the two accounts, even if one is consistent with the other, had strikingly contrasting implications when Sartre entered into the political and historical phase of his career. Beckett's drama led away from both politics and history at the very moment when Sartre was moving full speed in their direction. We shall begin with Beckett's play and Sartre's response. After that, we shall examine Sartre's second, politicized reading of the "human condition."

* * *

The kinship of *Waiting for Godot* with Sartre's original position on the human condition is unmistakable. "Our life is only a long waiting," Sartre had written in *Being and Nothingness.*[5] Five years earlier, in *Nausea,* he had offered some thoughts on the experience of waiting, understood as the human condition: "Nothing happens while you live. The scenery changes, people come in and go out, that's all. There are no beginnings. Days are tacked on to days without rhyme or reason, an interminable, monotonous addition…. Neither is there any end."[6] Images of waiting in Sartre's early works, waiting for nothing, waiting without respite or conclusion, were central to his growing fame. It was Samuel Beckett, however, who understood best how to place on the Parisian stage an unforgettable presentation of the Sartrean vision.[7]

One way to underscore Beckett's achievement as a dramatist is to note his success, arguably considerably greater than Sartre's, in combining form and content, medium and message. Where Sartre offered the audience a tidy plot in *The Flies,* Beckett deliberately shunned the same because a plot imposes coherence and meaning where there is none. All by itself, this distinction between plot and non-plot marks a noteworthy contrast; it is, however, only the first installment in a series of sharp contrasts between the stage of Sartre and that of Beckett.

The second installment may be seen in Beckett's decision to ignore classical literature. In the 1940s, Jean Anouilh dramatized the story of *Antigone,* Camus that of *Caligula,* Sartre that of Orestes in *The Flies.* These avant-garde intellectuals chose to take what was most old-fashioned in their education, their lessons in the classics, and to infuse new ideas into the old dramas: Sartre's Orestes has recourse to radical existentialist notions of freedom when he invites the furies to pursue him as he flees from Argos. Beckett, by contrast, deleted Greek myths and Roman history and invented a novel style of drama that was in perfect accord with the new ideas.

Not classical tragedy but modern comedy, Beckett understood, was fit for describing our pitiful condition: hence the three hats gag, Estragon's loss of his trousers, and other comic touches. Roquentin, discussing how we are *de trop,* remarked that "nothing existing can be comic," but he did draw an analogy "with certain aspects of vaudeville."[8] Beckett, Irish by birth, drew upon the cross-talk of Irish music hall vaudevillians when he wrote his play.[9] Where figures of royalty and aristocracy strode across the stage of Sartre (and Camus), Beckett placed on his vagabonds, bums, whose incessant pratfalls show that we are more comic than tragic beings.

What did the actions of the outsized heroes of antiquity—the violence perpetrated by Caligula, the murder of Aegistheus and Clytemnestra by Orestes—have in common with the undersized world of actual human beings? What had classical tragedy to do with a universe wherein all we do is wait for an appointment with Godot, knowing he will likely never show? However sad the fate of human beings, it is too small for tragedy. There is no greatness and therefore no tragedy in a world where the words of Beckett's Vladimir ring true: "We wait. We are bored.... We are bored to death.... In an instant all will vanish and we'll be alone once more, in the midst of nothingness!"[10]

While history has nothing to do with the human condition as understood by Beckett, time most certainly does. Time, the never-ending flow of time,[11] is the fundamental human reality. Placed at the center of Beckett's drama, time is why the recognition scenes of the classical theatre are replaced by a flurry of non-recognition scenes in *Waiting for Godot.* Oedipus comes to recognize that he has slept with his mother and killed his father, but the characters in Beckett's play repeatedly fail to recognize one another.[12] Indeed, they do not fully recognize themselves, lacking certainty they are the same today as they were yesterday. How could they be, given Sartre's formula that human reality "is what it is not and is not what it is."[13] Our very identity is ever at stake, since we never coincide with ourselves in a world marked by time.

Other parallels can be drawn between Beckett and the early Sartre. The root of a tree was enough to convince Roquentin of the absurdity of human existence; the "pus" of a tree and the "oozing" of all things natural lead Estragon to the same conclusion.[14] Beckett's characters bicker constantly, talk about parting company, but remain linked together—much as Sartre had characterized the relationship between self and other.[15] Unmistakably Sartrean, too, are Vladimir and Estragon's efforts to find something, anything, that will help them "pass the time" and "give us the impression we exist."[16]

Obviously, Sartre had many good reasons to be pleased with Beckett's play but, coming in 1953, Beckett was too late. The Sartre of 1938, of *Nausea*, might well have enthusiastically approved of *Waiting for Godot*, because both it and Sartre's novel taught the futility of action. "Nothing to be done"; "nothing you can do about it," say Beckett's characters; nothing more to do here, "nor anywhere else,"[17] which reminds us of Roquentin's statements that "one can't be a man of action," and "I don't want to do anything."[18] But by 1953, Sartre had charted a new course and was deeply involved in politics. There was no place for Beckett's reprise of the prewar Sartre in Sartre's postwar world of action. Like Sartre, Beckett had belonged to a Resistance group; but whereas Sartre in the postwar 1940s decided on a life of *engagement* and commitment, Beckett's message appeared to be one of political withdrawal.

To denounce a play that so faithfully dramatized his original philosophy was not Sartre's way of responding to Beckett. He preferred, instead, to undercut the influence of *Waiting for Godot*. Rather than dismiss Beckett's play as drama or as a presentation of his own understanding of the human condition, Sartre attacked it on political grounds. Only a few months after a very politically engaged Sartre published the *Critique of Dialectical Reason*, he complained that "Although *Godot* is certainly not a right-wing play, it represents a sort of universal pessimism that appeals to right-wing people."[19]

Simone de Beauvoir, too, if she rebuffed Beckett did so not on aesthetic or philosophical but on political grounds. Not immediately, however: in 1953, when the play Beckett began writing in the late 1940s was finally performed, her response was for the most part favorable: "I saw *Waiting for Godot*. I am always mistrustful of plays that use symbols to present the human condition in its universal aspect; but I was full of admiration at the way in which Beckett succeeded in captivating us."[20] Later, however, we find her denouncing the *Nouveau Roman* of Nathalie Sarraute in terms that make one wonder whether Beckett, mentioned in passing, continued to meet with her approval: "one of the constant factors of this whole school of writing is boredom; it takes all the savor, all the fire out of life, its impulse toward the future." There is nothing to be said, she added, for authors who ignore politics.[21]

Another device by which both de Beauvoir and Sartre dealt with the theme of waiting was to politicize and historicize it. Already in *The Second Sex*, years before *Waiting for Godot*, de Beauvoir had made such a move: "In a sense woman's whole existence is a waiting, … since her justification is always in the hands of an other.… She awaits the love, the gratitude, the praise of a husband or lover; she awaits from them her reasons to exist, her worth and even her being."[22] Similarly, Sartre in the mid-1950s wrote an essay on China in which he mentioned the "human condition" in passing before proceeding to make politics and history out of the experience of waiting. "Whenever they do not take control of History," Sartre contended, "the masses experience great events as periods of endless waiting." He then applied this lesson to China: "Between the circular time of old China and the irreversible time of new China, there is an intermediate phase, a gelatinous duration equally distant from History and repetition: the time of *waiting*." Closing these reflections on a high note, he wrote that "the thousand individual waits of the time of Repetition have come together and fused into a single hope."[23]

It is perhaps significant that Beckett was permitted to publish some of his work in *Les Temps Modernes*. Sartre could not bring himself either to embrace or to repudiate *Waiting for Godot*. To embrace it would have been to compromise his postwar efforts to convince the public that the message of "existentialism" was, despite the charges of his critics, far from being one of despair or nihilism. To repudiate it would have been to reject his own thought. Ignoring it while reminding the public that existentialism was a philosophy of action seemed the least objectionable course.

Yet he could never quite put *Waiting for Godot* out of his mind, as is implied by its brief appearance in the pages of his final major work, *The Family Idiot*. When offering his readers an insight into Flaubert as he was around 1850, Sartre repeatedly remarked that "Flaubert is waiting for Godot." Flaubert was "very near to Beckett's heroes: he waits, knowing it is to no purpose."[24] Apparently there is no reason to avoid citing Beckett's justly famous and undeniably Sartrean presentation of the human condition, provided one buries such comments in a maze of prose thousands of pages long.

Sartre could not, would not, and did not deny his rendering of the "human condition" in *Being and Nothingness*. His resolution was to move forward after the war while withdrawing nothing from his past, concentrating on presenting a reformulated version of the "human condition," one he deemed more compatible with his postwar efforts to immerse himself and his writings first in politics and then, eventually, in history.

* * *

It so happens that we have previously encountered Sartre's second presentation of the "human condition" as it emerged in the years immediately following World War II. All we need do is revisit publications such as "The Republic of Silence" and *Anti-Semite and Jew,* and the characteristics of his reconsidered understanding of the "human condition" should come into immediate focus.

We have noted that Sartre believed the French were denied a future for four years by the Germans and trapped in a self-perpetuating present and that under these adverse circumstances they were called upon to choose between either submission and "inauthenticity" or Resistance and "authenticity" (see Chapter 3). To the foregoing, we must now add his claim that the French came face-to-face during the Occupation, as never before, with "*la condition humaine.*" In "The Republic of Silence" Sartre wrote that "The often atrocious circumstances of our combat finally made it possible for us, without pretense or veil, to live in this mutilated and unsustainable situation that is called the human condition."[25] However brief Sartre's essay on torture and the Resistance, it permitted him to sustain the notion of the human condition while embedding it in politics and perhaps in history as well, if by "history" we allow the peculiar and temporary moment when history had been halted.

As with "The Republic of Silence," so with *Anti-Semite and Jew*: here, too, Sartre vindicated a revised notion of the "human condition" while incorporating political engagement and the idea of history denied. "What men have in common is not a 'nature' but a condition," he wrote in his pamphlet and then proceeded to judge anti-Semites and Jews by the standard of whether they were willing to face up to what is most fundamental in our existence. Without question, the anti-Semites fail the test: "Anti-Semitism is fear of the human condition"; it is a cowardly effort to escape from our condition by filling our emptiness with blind hatred and false claims of rootedness in the past.[26]

In the case of the Jews, Sartre's evaluation is more complicated, in that his account moved back and forth between the "human condition" and the much more specific exploration of the "situation" of the Jews. The former is "the ensemble of abstract characteristics common to all situations"[27] and applies to the Jews nonspecifically. The latter involves a description of the social situation of the Jews throughout the ages, especially in France. In the end, however, Sartre, wittingly or unwittingly, confounded the two categories by frequently speaking about the "Jewish condition" rather than the "Jewish situation."[28] Certainly his depiction of the "situation" of the Jews—one of perpetual anguish, torment, and anxiety—coincided perfectly with his account of the "human condition." Sartre had found a way to transform his thought into social commentary without leaving behind one of his most cherished conceptions, the "human condition."

Not least among the differences between Sartre's first version of the "human condition" and the second is that the "humanist" tradition, explicitly repudiated in *Nausea* and implicitly in *Being and Nothingness,* entered his thought after the war and stayed for the duration of his career. A human being, he had famously announced in *Being and Nothingness,* is merely a "useless passion,"[29] a formulation that would seem to outlaw humanism. When Sartre delivered his speech "Existentialism is a Humanism" in 1945, he reversed the position he had taken in his great philosophical treatise.

He also, in effect, withdrew the words found in his career-making novel, Beckett's dramatization of that novel, and one comment in *No Exit* (1944). In *Nausea,* paraphrasing Pascal, Roquentin demands, "What have you done with your humanism? Where is your dignity as a thinking reed?"[30] As for Beckett, the humanist belief in human dignity was implicitly denied, it has been argued, when he had his characters, time and again, leave the upright position, signifying the dignity of man.[31] For his part, Sartre repeatedly denied the claims of human dignity in his early works. When Garcin, entering a chamber in Hell, regrets the absence of a toothbrush, the Valet responds, "So you haven't yet got over your—what do you call it?—your sense of human dignity?"[32]

Roquentin, who "used to hang around some Parisian humanists,"[33] has nothing but contempt for the Self-Taught man, a humanist and a socialist, whom he encounters now and again at the library or a café. One of the many faults of humanists is that they think in universal terms, missing the individual person. Roquentin's response to the Autodidact's affection for a romantic couple seated near them at a restaurant is "You are not at all touched by them: you're touched by the Youth of Man, the Love of Man and Woman, the Human Voice."[34] Humanists also make the mistake of thinking that the answers to the puzzle of human existence can be found in the great books. And so it is that the Autodidact undertakes his foolish project, a kind of *studia humanitatis,* of reading all the books in the library, from A to Z. In *The Flies,* Orestes similarly learns that his classically educated tutor talks much but has nothing to say. We are well prepared for Roquentin's conclusion: "I *am not* a humanist."[35]

After the war, as Sartre formulated his second version of the "human condition," he reversed field, declaring that "existentialism is a humanism." The new Sartre was as eager to embrace the notion of human dignity as the old Sartre had been to deny the same: "Man is nothing else but that which he makes of himself. This is the first principle of existentialism.... What do we mean to say by this, but that man is of a greater dignity than a stone or a table?" Although he continued to assert that "man is condemned to be free," he now held that freedom was as much the greatness as the curse of humans.[36]

Courage and heroism also have their place in Sartre's renovated view of the "human condition." It was in particular from the experience of war that Sartre learned that heroism was not the monopoly of the few but was available to the many. Recalling his childhood, Sartre remarked that "What I preferred in pre-war heroism was its solitude and gratuitousness"—the opportunity it afforded a select few. This changed when he discovered that World War I "put heroism within reach of everyone."[37] During World War II, Sartre discerned additional links between warfare and the heroism of everyman. "What the drama of [World War II] gave me ... was the experience of heroism," he said in retrospect. "The militant in the Resistance who was caught and tortured became a myth for us."[38]

The foregoing words, uttered late in his career, inevitably take us back to his writings immediately following the close of the Second World War. Holding out against torture was a major theme of "The Republic of Silence" in 1944, of his play *Corpses without Shrouds* (*Morts sans sépulture*) in 1946, and was a topic of concern in *What Is Literature?*, 1947. With fierce determination Sartre insisted in "The Republic of Silence," and never tired of repeating the point, that "the secret of a man is not his Oedipus or inferiority complex ... : it is ... his power to resist torture and death."[39] Metaphorically when not literally, Jews continue to be tortured, he argued in his pamphlet on anti-Semitism, and there can be no doubt that in their case "authenticity demands much courage."[40]

Nothing better typified the human condition in Sartre's second version than torture, resistance, refusal, and saying "No." Or, to make the same point in terms borrowed from Kojève, we may repeat that Sartre sided with the "slave" (see Chapter 3). Soon, however, Sartre encountered a problem: the more he pondered Kojève's adaptations from Hegel, the less relevant they were. For while Kojève's talk about courageous slaves could be useful in addressing four years of history denied, he was useless for history affirmed. In the notes Sartre scribbled from 1947 to 1948, he penned this observation: "The Hegelian theory of the master and the slave is seductive as a phenomenology of human relations, but cannot stand up historically." Against Kojève, he noted that "it would be nice if history were the history of slaves but the fact is that slaves were ahistorical in antiquity." Medieval serfs, too, like ancient slaves, lived in a world of "pure repetition." It is "the men who are oppressors and who are free from repetition (lords and vassals) who are precisely historical in that they can freely link their past to their present through the outline of a future."[41] Kojève's slave rebellions, Sartre decided much later, might be the future (see Chapter 3) but were not the past.

Could Sartre somehow find a way to save his second account of the "human condition" once his concerns became reoriented toward the flow of history? How enthralled Sartre was with his second version of the human condition, especially the image of men and women tested by torture; how intent he was on saving his second version in his new world of historical consciousness, can be seen in *What Is Literature?* (1947). Here, on the one hand, is the Sartre who announced that, "brutally reintegrated into history, we had no choice but to produce a literature of historicity." At the same time, however, even as he moved forward, he revisited and expanded his previous treatment of torture, the experience that for four years was the centerpiece of history arrested. Why he looked back is clear: he did so because the question of how one would react to torture "carried us to the very frontiers of ourselves and of the human." The man being tortured "experiences his human condition to the bitter end." He could "choose only between abjection and heroism, that is, between the two extremes of the human condition."[42]

One of Sartre's objectives in *What Is Literature?* was to find an opening in the postwar period to reclaim the direct encounters with the human condition that had marked the period of the Occupation. The resumption of the flow of history might not be to his advantage in this situation, so he turned toward literature, issuing a call for "a literature of extreme situations." Not for him the previous generation of authors who had practiced "modest virtues"; not for him those earlier novelists who had "died with a good conscience without ever having explored their condition." His generation was to be entirely different: "we are all metaphysical writers" and "metaphysics is not a sterile discussion about abstract notions having nothing to do with experience. It is a living effort to embrace from within the human condition in its totality."[43]

In a footnote, Sartre named some of the authors of his day who dared address nothing less than the "human condition." "What are Camus, Malraux, Koestler, etc., now producing if not a literature of extreme situations? Their characters are at the height of power or in prison cells, on the eve of death or of being tortured or of killing. Wars, *coups d'état*, revolutionary action, bombardments, massacres.... On every page, in every line, it is always the whole man who is in question."[44]

Saint-Exupéry is also on Sartre's list of authors to admire, and his addition is important because it shows that violence and killing are perhaps less important to Sartre than a willingness to risk one's life even in times of peace. *Night Flight* involves not killings but the death of an aviator and the courage of a director on the ground to choose when to send a man on a mission under dangerous circumstances. Saint-Exupéry's novels about flight in its early heroic age are tragic and epic in tone. His aviators, he wrote, are "conquerors,"[45] not of their fellow men but of the mountains and plains beneath them—and of themselves.

Romanticism was linked to heroism in Sartre's sensibilities, and both to the "human condition." When, toward the end of his career, Sartre set about writing a biography of Flaubert, he displayed his hostility toward post-Romanticism (see Chapter 2). His attitudes toward Romanticism were quite different, as is especially evident in his writings decades earlier. In the course of advancing his second understanding of the "human condition," he had suffused his works with the ambiance of the Romanticism that preoccupied his childhood.[46] Heroism, courage, defiance, testing oneself in extreme situations—what are these if not Romantic themes? Romanticism, which dies hard if it dies at all, obliquely but forcefully manifested itself in the writings of the Sartre who emerged from the ashes of World War II. It is doubtful that his eventual immersion in a study of post-Romanticism marked the end of his attraction to Romanticism and quite certain that Romantic themes frequently infiltrated his earlier works whenever he addressed the "human condition."

The continuing resonance of Romantic themes was not, of course, the only reason Sartre had difficulty relinquishing the notion of a "human condition" even after it began to clash with his growing historicism and with his conviction that Camus had associated the term with political reaction. There was a rich French tradition of reflection on the "human condition" from which not even the most advanced twentieth-century thinkers could readily exempt themselves.

The "Human Condition" Yesterday and in Sartre's Day

In one fashion or another, Simone de Beauvoir almost always found herself in sympathy with the views set forth by Jean-Paul Sartre. Whatever was in his thought was likely to be in hers and vice-versa, because theirs was an intimate and symbiotic relationship. So even if our focus is on Sartre, it is worth noting how she began *The Ethics of Ambiguity,* published in 1947. Throughout the opening pages, she frequently spoke of the "human condition" and did so by calling on Montaigne and Pascal. Hegel appeared, too, but she was not about to permit the "human condition" of Montaigne and Pascal to be displaced by a troubling "optimism where even bloody wars simply express the fertile restlessness of the Spirit."[47] The *Essays* of Montaigne and the *Pensées* of Pascal are not so readily discarded.

For his part, Sartre throughout the years following the end of the Second World War frequently revisited the classic texts that addressed the "human condition" and obviously thought of himself as building on his illustrious predecessors. In *What Is Literature?,* it is true, he was contemptuous of the literary establishment of his day, which was irrelevant to the living by virtue of its sterile reverence for the dead; and which, in its praise of past masters, had "no intention of making Pascal and Montaigne more alive, but only of making Malraux and Gide more dead."[48] Sartre would reverse the procedure by calling on the dead to serve the living. One finds Pascal's name favorably cited many times in *What Is Literature?,*[49] and the same is still true of Sartre's final work, *The Family Idiot.*

Not Montaigne but Pascal was Sartre's man, no matter that it is in the *Essays* that one first encounters the expression that would inspire later French writers down to Sartre's own day: "Each man," wrote Montaigne, "carries the entire form of *the human condition.*"[50] Although there are passages in the *Essays* that might have met with Sartre's approval, or at least might have aroused him to comment one way or the other, he said nothing about them. "I do not portray being; I portray passing," wrote Montaigne, adding elsewhere "all contradictions may be found in me"—words that might well have resonated with Sartre. As might these: "We are all patchwork, and so shapeless and diverse in composition that each bit, each moment, plays its own game. And there is as much difference between us and ourselves as between us and others."[51] Nevertheless, Sartre was as quiet about Montaigne as he was voluble about Pascal.

Why the silence about Montaigne? One answer is that whatever overlap existed between Montaigne's message and Sartre's was obliterated by a fundamental clash of sensibilities. Montaigne took pleasure in his inconsistencies, his inner divisions, his need to write essays—attempts, soundings [*essayer*]—rather than systematic treatises because he could not find firm footing on which to make decisions.[52] To him, the very traits that to Sartre added up to a devastating portrayal of the human condition were, instead, part and parcel of the richness of his being, of humans in general, and an enticement to endless, joyful researches into the byways and detours of human existence.

There is another reason why Sartre held Montaigne at bay. On those relatively rare occasions when Sartre did cite the author of the *Essays*, it was Montaigne the skeptic who drew his attention[53]—and his ire. The thinker who in *Being and Nothingness* would not settle for phenomenology by itself but only as a method of arriving at a full-blown ontology; the thinker who in the *Critique of Dialectical Reason* set out to unravel the "the Truth of History" and to establish that "there is *one* human history, with *one* truth and *one* intelligibility"[54]—this thinker throughout his career consistently spurned skeptics and skepticism. So hostile was he to Montaigne that in *What Is Literature?*, where he seemingly could not invoke "the human condition" too often,[55] Sartre dismissed him out of hand with what verged on an *ad hominem* remark: "Montaigne's skepticism? Who can take it seriously since the author of the *Essays* got frightened when the plague ravaged Bordeaux?"[56]

Pascal fared as well in Sartre's writings as Montaigne fared poorly. As we have seen, Pascal appeared as early as *Nausea* where Roquentin paraphrases the entry in the *Pensées* that reads "Man is only a reed, the most feeble thing in nature, but he is a thinking reed." That entry in Pascal's notebooks is accompanied by another: "thought constitutes the grandeur of man."[57] In 1938, pursuing his original understanding of the human condition, Sartre has Roquentin question whether the thinking reed has dignity. But by 1945, when Sartre was working with his second understanding of the human condition, he came around to the Pascalian point of view. Consciousness was no longer understood in "Existentialism is a Humanism" solely as that which makes us the freaks of the universe, holes in being condemned ever to chase after ourselves; it was also designated the source of human dignity.

The year 1947 offers convenient markers by which we can discern the place of Pascal in Sartre's outlook. His notebooks for that year state his one misgiving about Pascal, the absence or even denial of the significance of history.[58] Yet even as Sartre's growing political commitments pulled him toward the study of history, he refused to dismiss Pascal from his reflections, going out of his way in those same notebooks to suggest that the author of the *Pensées* qualifies as still relevant to a twentieth-century atheist because he was not a true believer: "When Pascal writes: the eternal silence of these infinite spaces terrifies me, he speaks as an unbeliever, not as a believer."[59] *What Is Literature?*, in the same year, contains numerous references to Pascal,[60] none unfavorable, as when he cited Pascal's remark that it is impossible to tell where nature ends and custom begins[61]—to which we may add that

Sartre, perhaps tellingly, granted Montaigne no credit for having made the same point a century before Pascal.[62]

That between Sartre and Pascal there was an elective affinity is undeniable. "I am not a necessary being,"[63] reads an entry in the *Pensées* that sounds exactly like the Sartre of *Nausea* and *Being and Nothingness*. Again in advance of Sartre, Pascal held that everything that exists is contingent: "We burn with desire to find a firm footing, an ultimate lasting base on which to build a tower ... , but our whole foundation cracks and the earth opens up into the depth of the abyss."[64] Long before Roquentin proclaimed that nature is incoherent and that science cannot save us, Pascal had said the same. Science can discover neither final nor genetic causes, Pascal sighed, nor can it prove any necessary connection in the realm of efficient causes: "Who has demonstrated that there will be a tomorrow? ... It is habit that persuades us." Least of all can science comfort us in our misery without God or tell us how to live.[65]

It is difficult to believe that Sartre could have been ignorant of how closely Pascal's understanding of the human condition resembled his. The "condition of man" as defined by Pascal is one of "inconstancy, boredom, anxiety."[66] We must do something, anything to pass the time, as Beckett said in his dramatic presentation of Sartre's original version of the human condition. "Diversion" is a favorite word in *Waiting for Godot*,[67] and the same may be said of the *Pensées*. "Nothing could be more wretched than to be ... reduced to introspection with no means of diversion," thought Pascal. We cannot sit still, cannot bear to be without a diversion, because then we would have to concede our "nothingness."[68]

On the topics of the experience of time and the quest for self-knowledge, the stances of Pascal, although taken in the seventeenth century, are strikingly relevant to the twentieth-century speculations of Sartre. Obviously, Pascal did not develop a full-scale philosophy of time, as Heidegger and Sartre would three hundred years later; yet his reflections are worth mentioning. "We never keep to the present. We recall the past; we anticipate the future," and never are we "present" to ourselves. "Thus," concludes Pascal, "we never actually live, but only hope to live, and since we are always planning how to be happy, it is inevitable that we should never be so."[69] Sartre, in his first incarnation of the human condition, never put the matter more eloquently.

In regard to the search for self-knowledge, once again Montaigne and Pascal were numbered among the thinkers who preceded Sartre, with Pascal, as usual, stating the position that was closer to the one Sartre would eventually take. In a perfect statement of the principle of "privileged access,"

Montaigne wrote, "There is no witness so sure as each man to himself"[70]; which is to say, he adhered to the very position that Sartre the purveyor of existential psychoanalysis deemed highly problematic. Much closer to Sartre was Pascal's entry: "We are nothing but lies, duplicity, contradiction, and we hide and disguise ourselves from ourselves." Foremost among the obstacles to self-knowledge for both Pascal and Sartre but not Montaigne is that we do not want to know ourselves.[71]

It is true, of course, that we cannot be certain that every item in Pascal's thought which sounds Sartrean actually played a significant role in shaping the writings of Jean-Paul Sartre. What we do know on the basis of direct evidence is, however, quite significant. As early as *Nausea* and as late as his multivolume study of Flaubert, Pascal's name and explicit references to one or another Pascalian formulation make frequent appearances in Sartre's works. For instance, during the late 1940s, Sartre turned to Pascal not only in *What Is Literature?* but also in "Black Orpheus," his tribute to black poets in lands that had suffered "centuries of slavery." When "the black man goes back to his principal experience, it is suddenly revealed to him in two dimensions: it is both the intuitive seizure of the human condition and the still fresh memory of a historical past. Here, I am thinking of Pascal, who relentlessly repeated that man was an irrational composite of metaphysics and history."[72]

Into the 1960s and 1970s, Sartre continued to pay tribute to Pascal. His journalistic account of revolutionary Cuba features a reference to Pascal, along with a comment on the human condition in a new world: "what we are doing is nothing less than deciding on the human condition when we present it as if it were smothered in this world by inflexible laws; and, similarly, we are deciding on the human condition when we take our destiny into our own hands."[73] *The Family Idiot* of the early 1970s is not only a culmination of Sartre's thought; it is also an exercise in what Sartre termed "our linking of Flaubert and Pascal" and features a treasure trove of citations to Pascal. Among the famous passages of the *Pensées* that Sartre turned to his own advantage in re-creating Flaubert's world are these: Pascal on "diversion," "the wager," the "misery of man without God"; on participating in religious rituals not because one believes but in order to believe; plus numerous brief, incidental references to Pascal.[74] It is also worth remarking that sometimes Sartre surrounded an isolated allusion to Pascal with multiple references to "the human condition."[75]

When Sartre pondered the "human condition," Pascal was not the only one who accompanied him on his journey. Closer at hand, and explicitly acknowledged was André Malraux, author of, among other books, a novel bearing the title *La Condition Humaine*. As previously noted, Sartre pointed to Malraux's example when issuing a call in 1947 for a "literature of extreme situations." Eventually, of course, he would break with Malraux over politics. It was troubling that Malraux served as Charles de Gaulle's Minister of Information in the provisional government formed in November, 1945; it was unforgivable that in 1958, upon de Gaulle's return to power, Malraux accepted the post of Minister of Cultural Affairs.

The Malraux worth noting was the heroic adventurer who strode the earth and the world of letters from the 1920s to the end of the Second World War. How could Sartre not be drawn to the earlier Malraux whose formulations sometimes read in retrospect as if he were a godfather of existentialism, and whose version of the human condition might have offered Sartre a third variation, reaching beyond resistance, pointing toward revolution and fellow-traveling with the Communist party? Malraux had participated with and written about the Chinese revolutionaries of the 1920s and for many years flirted with the Communist party, just as Sartre would later, beginning in the 1950s.

The Walnut Trees of Altenburg was Malraux's final novel but remained incomplete because "the Gestapo destroyed too many pages for me to re-write it." Still, it was published unfinished in 1943 and is important, if for no other reason than because it sounds at moments like a literary expression of existentialism before its triumph. One passage in particular, in this regard, stands out: "The greatest mystery is not that we should have been thrown here at random between the profusion of matter and that of the stars, but that in this prison we can draw from ourselves images powerful enough to deny our nothingness."[76]

In 1967, Malraux wrote "What interests me in any man is the human condition."[77] Testing oneself against the threat of death, defining oneself in extreme circumstances, facing up to our nothingness, had been the favorite themes of his earlier literary explorations, nowhere more so than in *La Condition Humaine,* his novel of 1933. At one point or another in the novel, Malraux briefly sounded themes that would later be central to Sartre's starting point: nausea, anguish, the hardness or softness of flesh, the "other" looking at and judging me. One also finds ample notions of heroism and human dignity, which would often figure in Sartre's writings of the immediate postwar era.[78]

Perhaps the single most important passage in *La Condition Humaine,* from Sartre's perspective, is an account of a Chinese revolutionary awaiting his turn to be executed: "He was dying, like each of these men, because he had given a meaning to his life. What would have been the value of a life for which he would not have been willing to die? It is easy to die when one does not die alone." Earlier in the novel, the reader had listened to a character who was unable to identify with others and felt fated, if he sacrificed himself, to die alone; near the end the very different theme is one of belonging and dying together, which is to say that within the pages of a single novel Malraux had charted a journey Sartre would later replicate over several years as his thought moved from an emphasis on solitude to solidarity.[79] It is not surprising that in 1947 Sartre should write that "whereas we needed the urgency and the physical reality of a conflict in order to discover ourselves, Malraux had the immense merit of recognizing as early as his first work that we were at war."[80]

There was, of course, one more author whose rendition of the "human condition" Sartre admired, a contemporary praised by him for his noteworthy contributions to the literature of "extreme situations," and that was Albert Camus. Before the bitter quarrel that broke out between them when Camus published *The Rebel,* each of the two men had expressed appreciation of the other's literary creations. Camus had praised *Nausea* and the short story "The Wall"; Sartre, for his part, did not hesitate to say, "I read *The Plague,* by Camus, and loved it."[81]

Camus's novel appeared in 1947 at the very moment when its dual message fit perfectly into Sartre's evolving sensibilities. One meaning, which matched well with Sartre's original understanding of the human condition, was that "we all have plague"; which is to say, insofar as we are all condemned to die, "each of us has the plague within him." And Sartre must have thought of his own words in *Being and Nothingness* when he read Camus's sentence, "the whole town seemed like a railway waiting-room."[82]

In his images of death, Camus effectively recapitulated Pascal, and, in effect if not in intent, rewrote one of the most famous entries found in the *Pensées:* "Imagine a number of men in chains, all under sentence of death, some of whom are each day butchered in the sight of the others; those remaining see their own condition in that of their fellows, and looking at each other in grief and despair await their turn. This is an image of the human condition." Thus spoke Pascal whose echo may be found in the voice of Camus's narrator: the residents of Oran, he reports at the end of the story, had been "that bewildered people a part of which was daily fed into a furnace … while the rest, in shackled impotence and fear, awaited their turn."[83]

Sartre, it will be recalled, had vigorously attacked "humanism" in *Nausea* and then, after the war, reinstated it on his own terms. Camus did the same in *The Plague*. At first he ridiculed humanism: the townsfolk of Oran "were humanists: they disbelieved in pestilences. A pestilence isn't a thing made to men's measure." They believed it would pass away, but it was they who passed away "and the humanists first of all, because they haven't taken their precautions." Eventually, however, it becomes obvious that the main character, Doctor Rieux, is indeed a humanist, albeit one who has no use for the optimism, illusions, and belief in progress of nineteenth-century humanism.

Even Sartre's recovery of heroic ideals immediately after the war finds its counterpart in Camus's novel, the only difference being that Dr. Rieux's heroism is muted: "there's no heroism in all this," he writes, "it's a matter of common decency." But we, of course, know better. The reader is well aware that the good doctor and his compatriots have risked their lives to fight the plague; the reader also recognizes—and here is Camus's second meaning—that the plague is a metaphor for the Nazi Occupation and that the sanitation squads are the Resistance movement.

In the late 1940s, Sartre and Camus appeared to be in perfect accord in their understanding of the human condition, both in its metaphysical and its political significations. It was only right that at this moment Camus should have initiated Sartre to journalism, and that Sartre should have reciprocated by inviting Camus to assist in one of his plays. No one could have anticipated that the two friends would soon become bitter enemies or that their fight would raise the question of whether studies of human history and of the human condition are compatible.

The Camus Factor

The break between Sartre and Camus came in 1951 with the publication of *L'Homme Révolté*, or *The Rebel*, Camus choosing a position that was liberal in all but name, Sartre siding at the same time with revolution and the Soviet Union. So impassioned was the response of Sartre and his comrades on *Les Temps Modernes* that we forget how much the two writers had in common before the Cold War divided them. Remembering how much the two writers shared before their conflict adds insight into the intensity of Sartre's hostile reaction. There was a sense on Sartre's part that he had been betrayed by someone whose intellectual trajectory closely mimicked his own.

A great deal of thematic overlap is evident in the early works of Sartre and Camus. The notion that human existence is "absurd" is common to *Nausea* and *The Myth of Sisyphus* (1942),[84] and the claim that we are *de trop* figures both in *Nausea* and *The Stranger* (1942).[85] Similarly, just as Sartre declared in 1943 that it makes no difference whether one gets drunk alone or is a leader of nations, Camus wrote a year before that "one life was as good as another," meaning that "all experiences are unimportant," all choices equally arbitrary.[86] One may also detect an affinity between Sartre's philosophy of consciousness and Camus's statement, "Beginning to think is beginning to be undermined."[87]

Among the similarities between Sartre and Camus in the early 1940s is this: each man's writings and life displayed a striking disunity of theory and practice. So far as theory is concerned, Sartre in *Being and Nothingness* depicted the human condition in most dire terms, and the same is true of Camus's *The Myth of Sisyphus*; yet each author was at the same time moving toward political engagement: in Camus's case as an editor of the Resistance newspaper *Combat*; in Sartre's as supporter of the Resistance and initiator of a postwar political movement. Indeed, as Simone de Beauvoir's account shows,[88] Sartre had always had sympathies for the left, no matter what his formal philosophy might dictate. Likewise, it was a sign of Camus's youthful attraction to political radicalism, briefly to the Communist party, that in *Sisyphus* he purloined the expression "permanent revolution" from anarchists and Marxists (see Chapter 5) and applied it to the apolitical, everyday life of persons facing up to the absurd: "The theme of permanent revolution is carried into individual experience."[89]

By the late 1940s, Sartre had moved to a second, politicized formulation of the "human condition," and Camus's novel, with its allegory of fighting against the Nazis, did the same. For both men, Resistance was the perfect exemplar of their new understanding of the human condition; for both, it was the moment when their theory caught up with their practice. Four years later, however, when Sartre sided with the Communist party, he would surely have balked at the portions of Camus's novel that came down hard not on the Nazis but on the Communists. Sartre "loved" *The Plague* in 1947; had it been published four years later, he very likely would have hated it.

One of the admirable characters in *The Plague* is Rambert, a journalist reporting (as Camus himself did) on the plight of the Arabs, who is trapped in Oran when the plague strikes. Separated from his lover, Rambert schemes to escape from quarantine to rejoin her. But, when granted the long awaited opportunity to leave, he declines: "I belong here whether I want it or not. This business is everybody's business." Rambert fights the good fight in Oran, at risk of death, as he had in Spain during the Civil War. He does so, however, while adamantly abjuring ideological justifications: "I've seen enough of people who die for an idea."[90] The plague is the "abstraction,"[91] as is Communist ideology, and no one should die for an abstraction.

Tarrou is the tormented figure in the novel who joined the Communists to combat the plague, only to discover that he was spreading the disease in the name of fighting it. Although he leaves the party, he does not suppress the impulses that had drawn him there in the first place. "What interests me is learning how to become a saint," he tells Dr. Rieux; he wants to be "a saint without God," and by aiming so high he assures his own misery. The doctor by contrast, who is Camus's man, "feels more fellowship with the defeated than with saints." Modesty, moderation, and quiet dedication rather than ideological fervor mark the life of the doctor: "Salvation's much too big a word for me. I don't aim so high. I'm concerned with a man's health; and for me his health comes first."[92]

Why Sartre endorsed *The Plague* in *What Is Literature?* while saying nothing about Camus's attack on Communism and revolutionary politics is not entirely clear. Possibly he missed what was, after all, only a subplot in the novel. Or, more likely perhaps, Sartre simply did not care because in 1947 he was trying to forge a middle way between capitalism and Communism, America and Russia.[93] But by 1951, when *The Rebel* appeared, Sartre was in the throes of his most ardent fellow-traveling, which culminated in his defense of the Communist party in *The Communists and Peace.* No longer could he afford to look the other way. Camus and his message had to be repudiated, vigorously, uncompromisingly; and Sartre's cohort set about the task, sparing neither Camus the man nor Camus the author.

After the dust had settled, at least one important question remained to be answered. Where, under the new dispensation, did talk of the "human condition" stand in Sartre's outlook? Was there still a chance that he might move on from his second version, tied to the Resistance and history arrested, to a third version, linked to revolution and seizure of the future? Or would Camus's insistence on pitting the "human condition" against historicism lead Sartre to abandon discussions of the human condition in the course of vindicating historicism and the revolutionary cause?

* * *

Before the publication of *The Rebel,* Sartre continued to mention the "human condition" at the same time that he sought to come to terms with history and historicism. Camus, however, attempted to force a choice between the "human condition" and historicism—one or the other, he insisted, not both. "Purely historical thought is nihilistic," he announced, and in his concern to find something permanent, changeless, ahistorical, he reinstated the old notion of human nature. "The rebel, far from making an absolute of history, rejects and disputes it, in the name of a concept that he has of his own nature." Against the postulates of the day, Camus affirmed that "a human nature does exist, as the Greeks believed."[94] Existence, apparently, does not precede essence.

While he never defined "human nature," Camus appeared to use that term interchangeably with the expression "human condition." As in *The Myth of Sisyphus,* our condition is that we are fated to die; our best response is nonpolitical rebellion, refusing to submit, striving to fill the void with artistic creation and a life lived to the fullest. The new note in *The Rebel* is Camus's recognition that our human condition is one we hold in common, and the acknowledgment that if life is good for one person it is good for all: "I rebel—therefore we exist."[95] Murder, especially the mass murder of totalitarian regimes is reprehensible, no matter that the slaughter is carried out in the name of generations to come.

The present should never be sacrificed to the future, Camus held in *The Rebel,* a position that did not require him to rethink his earlier work. In *The Myth of Sisyphus,* he had held that "the present and the succession of presents before a conscious soul is the ideal of the absurd man." Likewise Meursault, the protagonist of *The Stranger,* remarked that he had always been "absorbed in the present moment." Only in *The Plague* did Camus sound a slightly different note, and then only temporarily, when he has Doctor Rieux lament that "nothing was left us but a series of present moments." *The Rebel* reaffirms and politicizes his typical stand, that the present should be our sole concern. Near the end of Camus's anti-revolutionary polemic, as a concluding thought, he wrote "real generosity toward the future lies in giving all to the present."[96]

Camus thought *The Rebel* his best book. One need not be a Sartrean to disagree with him on this point. Among the glaring weaknesses of his performance was his insistence, in keeping with other Cold War liberals, on interpreting Communism as secularized religion, as if commitment to the party was fundamentally a matter of trying to find a substitute for God and the absolute. Marxism, he assures us, is a "horizontal religion," its writings are "the Scriptures" of "the Fathers," its science a form of "Messianism," its forecasts "prophecy," its followers await "the advent of the proletarian

Christ." The proletariat is charged with a "mission," which is nothing less than through their sufferings to act as "Christ in human form redeeming the collective sin of alienation." Relentlessly pursuing his argument by analogy, Camus declared that "Russian Communism has appropriated [a] metaphysical ambition … : the erection, after the death of God, of a city of man finally deified." Weakness, cowardice, unwillingness to face up to the absurdity of human existence, in Camus's view, account for membership in the party. "Man takes refuge in the permanence of the party in the same way that he formerly prostrated himself before the altar."[97]

The foregoing interpretation, no matter how often it was repeated by Cold War liberals, does not stand up to critical scrutiny. It was not the search for a new deity but the execution of his brother at the hands of the Czar's police that led Lenin to become a Marxist revolutionary. How, moreover, can anyone take seriously the thought that Stalin's purges were based on religious urges, or that the large postwar vote for Communists in Italy and France had anything to do with the search of workers for a new faith? Perhaps some intellectuals were attracted to "the God that failed," but the agenda of the workers was based on economic want, sometimes manifested by a vote of protest in favor of the Communist party.

In the pages of *Les Temps Modernes,* Sartre and his colleague Francis Jeanson wrote withering responses to *The Rebel.* Jeanson struck first and last, before and after Sartre's polemical rejoinder. Central to Jeanson's critique was his attack on Camus's efforts to substitute discussion of the "human condition" for much needed historical analysis. The problem, Jeanson charged, was already evident in *The Plague.* Were it not for Malraux's *La Condition Humaine,* Camus might have issued his book under that title, remarked Jeanson, so central is the idea of the "human condition" in his novel. But whereas Malraux immersed his book in history, Camus's novel, unfortunately, "recounted events as seen from on high, by a nonsituated subjectivity." The problem is exacerbated in *The Rebel* because there Camus "eliminates all concrete situations in order to obtain a pure dialogue of ideas." To the extent that Camus bothers with history, he does so only "to be done with history," "to detach himself from history from within history," which is an exercise in futility and irresponsibility.[98]

When Jeanson hit his foe a second time, he seemingly could not cite Camus's references to the "human condition" too often,[99] always to accuse him of missing our real, historical condition. Camus's rebellion against the Christian God leaves the world as it is, commented Jeanson with disgust. Revolutionaries and workers Camus fails to understand and "ascribes to them a [religious] project they don't have and neglects to mention their real [economic] motivations."[100]

Sartre's polemical response to Camus bears a close resemblance to Jeanson's but is perhaps more harsh. Where Jeanson had spoken of "eternal France," the motto of the reactionaries, without accusing Camus of aligning with the far right, Sartre did not hesitate to write "you have become a counter revolutionary." As for Camus's philosophy of nonviolence, it denied in advance the possibility that he could deal effectively with the war in Indochina. Camus cared for the "human condition" when the true issue was "our *historical* condition." Every worker knew what Camus ignored, that "the absurdity of our condition is not the same in [affluent] Passy as in [impoverished] Billancourt." "You rebelled against death, but in the industrial belts that surround cities, other men rebelled against social conditions."[101]

Sartre's evolving theme and variation on Camus as heir to the classical French *moralistes,* famous for their insights into the "human condition," is revealing. Initially, when he reviewed *The Stranger* in 1943, Sartre complimented Camus on belonging to this tradition, which culminated, he held, in Nietzsche. In 1952, however, after the publication of *The Rebel,* Sartre altered his position: "you remain within our great classical tradition which, since Descartes, and with the exception of Pascal, had been completely hostile to history." Eight years later, following Camus's death in 1960, Sartre tried to be more conciliatory but remained highly ambivalent: Camus, he observed, "represented in this century, and against History, the present heir to that long time line of *moralistes* whose works perhaps constitute what is most original in French letters."[102]

Had the discussion of the "human condition" survived Sartre's quarrel with Camus? According to Sartre's former ally, now his dangerous enemy, a choice had to be made: the human condition or human history. Clearly Camus chose the former; did Sartre feel compelled to answer by choosing the latter or did he continue, somehow, to adhere to both?

Less Than Final Thoughts

Before *The Rebel,* and especially in the years immediately following the Second World War, from 1945 to 1947, Sartre self-consciously sought a synthesis of two discourses, two intellectual traditions, one dealing with the older notion of the "human condition"; the other with the newer historicist mentality.

Les Temps Modernes was explicitly dedicated to the idea of the writer who acknowledged his place in history, the better to change the world rather than merely resist it. It is perhaps surprising, then, to see the strong emphasis on "the metaphysical condition" of humans in the introductory essay Sartre wrote in 1945 for the new collective publication. "We have little taste for the purely historical," he remarked. "Each age discovers an aspect of the human condition; in every era man chooses himself in confrontation with other individuals, love, death, the world." Historicists were invited by Sartre in 1945 both to generalize within a period and also to address the commonalities of all periods; and they could do so, Sartre maintained, while still remaining faithful to their method: "by taking part in the singularity of our era, we ultimately make contact with the eternal, and it is our task as writers to allow the eternal values implicit in such social or political debates to be perceived."[103]

A year later, 1946, Sartre wrote that "man is always the same, facing a situation which is always changing."[104] Then in 1947, he published *What Is Literature?*, which brims with allusions to the "human condition" at the same time that Sartre affirms our historicity. History itself, he argued in this work, proved why we must not forego the notion of the human condition: "The war and the Occupation, by precipitating us into a world in a state of fusion, perforce made us rediscover the absolute at the heart of relativity itself." Also noteworthy is an entry in his notebooks of the late 1940s: "no doubt a universal does exist. But it itself is lived out historically."[105]

Even in 1952, the year of his impassioned denunciation of *The Rebel,* Sartre made favorable references to the "human condition" on a number of occasions in his book on Jean Genet. As in his earlier work, Sartre continued to speak of "the absolute of the human condition" and suggested that the shortcoming of young Genet was that "he wanted to transcend the human condition, and was in consequence relegated to a level below humanity." What is most remarkable is Sartre's continuing praise of *The Myth of Sisyphus.* In particular, Sartre in his study of Genet commended Camus's skill in portraying "some of the trivial experiences which sometimes reveal to us the fundamental absurdity of our condition."[106]

One might try to make the case that historicism eventually triumphed over the human condition in Sartre's thought by pointing to the *Critique of Dialectical Reason.* When in volume two we finally come upon a mention of the "human condition," the entry in question is lonely and insignificant, stranded in the middle of the volume, swallowed up in a sea of surrounding words.[107] Yet the absence of the "human condition" from the *Critique* does not prove that Sartre abandoned it in his more "mature" reflections, for in truth, it continued to appear in a great many of Sartre's works after his confrontation with Camus and never took its leave. Most significant in this regard, presumably, are the plentiful references in *The Family Idiot,* published some twenty years after *The Rebel,* and a work of mature historical reason.

Throughout the three enormous volumes of *The Family Idiot,* Sartre repeatedly accused Flaubert of striving to "escape from" the human condition and his fellow Post-Romantics of attempting to "rise above" it. Foolishly, the artists of Flaubert's day made the mistake of "rejecting the human condition in order to escape from the bourgeois condition," which rendered them harmless, much to the delight of the social class they hated. Another charge lodged by Sartre against Flaubert was that he exercised a "will to fall below the human condition."[108] Speaking so often and so favorably of the notion of the "human condition," Sartre found himself in his study of Flaubert, decades after their falling out, uttering favorable comments on Camus, especially his *The Myth of Sisyphus.*[109] Never, it is true, did Sartre explicitly formulate a full-fledged third version of the "human condition" in accordance with his politics of Revolution as opposed to Resistance. Nevertheless references to "the human condition" permeate his later works.

We may conclude that, however far Sartre moved into the intellectual camp of historicism, however much Camus strove to force the editors of *Les Temps Modernes* to choose between the human condition and human history, Sartre was never shy about appealing to the "human condition." There was, however, one important change over the years. Whereas Sartre in his writings of the early postwar years outspokenly struggled with the problem of how to reconcile the unchanging human condition with changing human history, those discussions disappear in his later thought. He simply dodged the question, slipping matters concerning the human condition into his writings whenever he pleased without acknowledging a problem to be resolved.

There is a resolution we might offer in his behalf. Sartre in his late years as a writer, before illness overtook him, sought to employ a revised method of thinking in an essay of 1964 on Kierkegaard and in his massive study of Flaubert. His intention was to set forth an account of Kierkegaard (or Flaubert) as a "singular universal," with all history running through his subject and his subject reaching out to all of history. As Dilthey had wished, biography and universal history, unique adventure and totalization, would be one. History and the transcendence of historicity would also be one. "Each of us, in our very historicity, escapes History to the extent that we make it," he wrote in his commentary on Kierkegaard. "I myself am historical to the extent that others also make history and make me, but I am a trans-historical absolute by virtue of what I make of what they make of me."[110]

What for Sartre was the "human condition" in his final thought if not the manner in which an individual human being is conditioned by the burdensome weight of historical reality but still makes choices of how to live his or her own life at this time, in this situation? And what is "history" if not an account of the outcome of those choices? Freedom never exited Sartre's discussion of the human condition, no matter how many concessions he felt compelled to make to unfreedom.

Quite possibly, Sartre's comments on Kierkegaard are the functional equivalent—and plausibly a noteworthy extension—of his discussions of the late 1940s on the intersection of human history and the human condition. Whether Sartre thereby solved the problem is, admittedly, far from clear.

Chapter 5

History and Revolution

Almost from the beginning and definitely to the end, the study of history for Sartre was overwhelmingly the study of revolution. Immediately after World War II, he became fascinated with groups denied a heritage, trapped in the present, sadly denied a future but thankfully denied the opportunity to lose themselves in the past. This preoccupation with cultures destroyed and time frozen is never entirely absent from his more mature postwar writings (see Chapter 3), but soon it yielded ground to another stream of thought. Through his political activism and his writing of history, Sartre from the 1950s to the end of his days—and posthumously—sought to claim the future for the wretched of the earth. Revolution, not merely resistance, henceforth would be his overriding concern. Having decided to devote the rest of his life to furthering the cause of revolution, he quite naturally found himself increasingly dedicated to studying the history of revolutions, those of times past, those still in the making, those that might yet come to pass.

Perhaps inevitably, as Sartre plunged deeper and deeper into the question of revolution, he found himself engaged in an ongoing debate with the spokespersons, past and present, of the rich tradition of European revolutionary thought. By no means were his battles solely with the "vulgar Marxists" of the French Communist party. The larger picture is that his accounts of history always have as a backdrop the nineteenth and twentieth century struggles of Marxists with anarchists over what history teaches about revolution.

Scholars have done well to spend so much time on the relationship of existentialism to Marxism in Sartre's *Critique of Dialectical Reason* and other works. There is, however, another matter to which we should attend, and that is the prominence in his historical works of contributions, sometimes oblique, often direct, to long-standing contests between Marxist and anarchist fomenters and interpreters of revolution. Behind the words printed on the pages of Sartre's books, one can spot, on a closer look, images of the black and red flags of his revolutionary predecessors and contemporaries, black the color of the anarchists, red of the Communists.

The Unwritten History of Liberalism

Sometimes the books that an author does not write are as revealing as his or her publications. In Sartre's case, there was every reason to suppose that he would offer a comprehensive account of the liberalism he repudiated—its liberal capitalist economy, its liberal politics, its liberal ideology. Even if, as is true, he placed his emphasis on writing the history of revolutionary politics, he and his readers might well have benefited from a full-scale history of the liberal enemy he never tired of excoriating, not least because it stood in the way of revolution.

Despite the many hits at liberalism strewn throughout Sartre's works—the many pieces of what might have been integrated into a comprehensive historical indictment—he never embarked on a history of liberalism. Perhaps the closest Sartre ever approached to filling this gap in his thought was *The Communists and Peace.* There, he did make a concerted effort to understand the peculiarities of French capitalism and liberalism, the reasons why the French case was eccentric—but never did he explain what was central to liberalism in Europe and America. It is not surprising that some of Sartre's most sympathetic and Marxist-leaning readers have expressed astonishment that the history of liberal capitalism is absent from the two volumes of the *Critique of Dialectical Reason.* "What is missing," writes Fredric Jameson, is capitalism "as a central actor on the stage of world history, as a primary agent, rather than a background system."[1]

Only the history of revolution, never the history of reform, interested Sartre. The first volume of the *Critique* devoted many pages to the French Revolution. Of the 456 pages of the unfinished second volume, nearly half deal with Russia, the Trotsky-Stalin struggle, and Stalinism. When "reform," a word frequently dear to liberal hearts, appears in volume two, it is in a passage lauding the "*reformist* praxis"[2] of the Communist party—reform in the service of revolution, not meliorism; in other words, to purloin words written in 1956, the only reform Sartre sanctioned was the restoration of "Marxism such as it is" to "Marxism such as it should be."[3]

Liberalism, which was originally on the agenda of the second volume of the *Critique,* was removed by Sartre, ostensibly because it is easier to deal with "the less complex structures" of what he calls "directorial societies" than with the more "complex" example of "bourgeois democracies."[4] Setting aside the question of whether his excuse is convincing, we may note that his decision to omit liberal societies from his work has come back to haunt him. When the postwar exile of French liberalism ended in the 1970s, the new generation of intellectuals who repudiated Soviet Russia and condemned fellow-travelers deemed Sartre a rich target. Because Sartre had charged that "liberalism is an ignoble word,"[5] his reputation declined precipitously, and one is left to ponder why he failed to do more by way of setting forth his version of the history of liberalism.

* * *

There is no doubt as to how Raymond Aron would explain Sartre's failure to subject liberalism to a sustained historical inquiry. To Aron, this would constitute one more proof that Marxism was in France "the opium of the intellectuals,"[6] revolution their fixation, liberalism their object of obsessive loathing and contempt. Certainly Maurice Merleau-Ponty, in the earlier phase of his thought, with his emotional longing for revolution, provided ample grist for Aron's mill: "Marxism is not *a* philosophy of history; it is *the* philosophy of history, and to renounce it is to dig the grave of Reason in history,"[7] he wrote in *Humanism and Terror* (1947). Sartre sounded somewhat similar when he remarked in 1956 that "if the U.S.S.R. is worth neither more nor less than capitalist England, then, indeed, not much is left to us but to cultivate our garden."[8] The romance of revolution militated against a serious treatment of liberalism.

So did the moribund state of liberalism in France, where the liberal persuasion fell into disgrace during the Occupation. Distinguished historian Daniel Halévy, for example, although the scion of a family of Orleanist liberals, had become so disenchanted with the Third Republic that he initially identified with Vichy's message of family, country, and return to the land. Not only the right-wingers but also the liberals emerged from the war thoroughly discredited by collaboration. One should not be astonished, therefore, to hear Sartre in the 1950s speak of "the death of bourgeois thought" or proclaim that "at the first contact with Marxism, bourgeois ideas die without the Marxists having to lift a finger."[9]

Very likely Sartre's quarrel with Camus reinforced his conviction of the irrelevance of liberalism. Over the course of the 1950s and 1960s, Sartre reached out to China, Algeria, Cuba, Africa. How provincial, then, must Camus's perspective have seemed. In *The Rebel,* Camus had announced that "the problem of rebellion has no meaning except within our own Western society" and that "the history of rebellion is inseparable from the history of Christianity." At the very moment when it was necessary to understand unfamiliar lands, Camus refused to look beyond the West.[10]

Sartre had no trouble dispatching Camus's ahistorical attempt, at the end of *The Rebel,* to run away from History by embracing Nature. Raymond Aron's liberal challenge to Sartre was far more formidable than Camus's because it flowed from the German historicism common to Aron and Sartre. It was Aron who studied in Germany as a young man and, upon his return to Paris, excited Sartre by telling him "if you are a phenomenologist, you can talk about this cocktail and make philosophy of it!"[11] Long before Sartre started down the road of historical thought, Aron had written a book on German sociology and another on the philosophy of history that also owed much to his German education.[12]

Eventually the divide between the two thinkers came down to Aron saying that, if forced to choose, he would side with America, while Sartre said he would side with Russia.[13] But much earlier in their relationship, it was already clear that Sartre would never listen to his erstwhile companion and fellow founding editor of *Les Temps Modernes.* Aron's unforgiveable sin was the link he drew between historicism and skepticism on behalf of liberalism. Writing against Sartre, Aron held that "the more that understanding the past expresses the historicity of the historian, ... the less it avoids perspectivism."[14] Quite typical of Sartre, in direct contrast, was the disgust he expressed for "instrumentalist perspectivism" in his 1956 commentary on Pierre Hervé's book criticizing the Communist party. The divide between Sartre and Aron was similar to the issues that eventually separated Sartre from Merleau-Ponty. "I have always considered, and still consider the Truth to be a whole," Sartre wrote in his eulogy of the thinker who had taught him the ins and outs of Marxist historicism. "Merleau-Ponty, on the contrary, found his security in a multiplicity of perspectives."[15] In a show of respect for the departed, Sartre diplomatically failed to mention that when Merleau-Ponty downgraded Marxism to one truth among others, he also chose to advocate a "new liberalism."[16]

Sartre simply would not abide any argument denying there is one historical truth because matters of epistemology were not all that was at stake. Politics weighed at least as heavily on his mind. Not for him the liberalism of truths but no Truth, of pluralism and tolerance. Simone de Beauvoir succinctly summarized the position she and Sartre shared: "Truth is one, error multiple. It is not an accident if the Right professes pluralism."[17]

Sartre ignored Aron,[18] just as he ignored all thinkers who found ways of transforming skepticism into pluralism and liberalism. He shrugged off without comment Aron's various critiques of the political and historical works of existential Marxists, critiques that Aron did not stop writing until he published a book dissecting the *Critique of Dialectical Reason.*[19] Wanting nothing to do with Aron's liberal skepticism derived from German sources, Sartre was equally resistant to the combination of skepticism and liberalism that could be unearthed from homegrown French sources, most notably Montaigne, who had put his philosophical skepticism to work in combating the ideological fanaticism of his day, the wars of religion. No wonder that Sartre was so much more receptive to Pascal than to Montaigne (see Chapter 4).

Finally, what should come as no surprise, Sartre turned his back on the skeptical liberalism of mid–twentieth century English liberal philosophers. Seemingly Sartre never moved beyond his youthful scorn for English philosophy, as recorded by Simone de Beauvoir: "I accepted, with some amusement, his comparison of English cooking and Locke's empiricism, both of which, he explained, were founded upon the analytical principle of juxtaposition."[20] Sartre might have amplified the joke by pointing out that while he was beating the drum for a literature of "extreme situations," the English philosophers were embellishing their works with homely analogies drawn from cooking, English cooking, chosen precisely because it was bland and boring.

Sartre would, of course, have had nothing but contempt for A. J. Ayer, whose reduction of knowledge to empirical and formal truths was, in political terms, an excuse for ending all debate about ethics and matters political, anything concerning ends rather than means. This was a liberalism of empirical and incremental entrapment. But there was also a far more expansive development of English philosophical liberalism that developed during Sartre's lifetime, voiced by Isaiah Berlin among others, which postulated that the irreducibility of ends to empirical fact or logical deduction meant that debate could and should flourish and never end. The philosophy of ordinary language, moreover, even if it began with present day usage, was increasingly about mutating meanings over time; it became historicism, the exploration of possibilities, ethical and political. Berlin insisted, however, on what Sartre would never concede, that grand dialogue "can be pursued consistently only in a pluralist ... society."

Extending an olive branch to France, Berlin expressed appreciation of what "the existentialists have taught us,"[21] namely, that study of society, politics, and history can never be *Wertfrei*. Sartre did not return the favor. Apparently he never bothered to inform himself about English developments, and, even if he had, would have rejected yet another alliance of skepticism, historicism, and liberalism.

If Sartre sidestepped what was most formidable in the theory of liberalism, he was little better at unraveling the intricate layers of its practice. Usually he contented himself with a hit at "liberal hypocrisy"[22] or some other slur similar in kind, to show that the practice of liberalism belied its theory. We should, however, remember the one occasion, early on, when Sartre made a case that liberal ideals were inadvertently undermining the liberal cause and that a revised liberalism might offer a worthy solution. In *Anti-Semite and Jew,* he warned that when liberals place the Jews under the general rubric of "Man" and champion their rights as Man, the Jews lose their identity and become more vulnerable to attacks from the right. Only a "concrete liberalism" will do, one that recognizes the rights of Jews as Jews and protects their group against others. This was the one occasion on which Sartre said something favorable about liberalism, but even in this instance, a mere three pages later, he forgot about liberalism, proclaiming that socialism is the answer to the Jewish and all social questions.[23]

In ignoring liberalism, Sartre arguably put himself inadvertently at odds with Karl Marx and Marxists. The volumes of *Das Kapital* were grounded in a deep reading of the liberal political economists, the better to prove that a fundamental social and political transformation was inevitable as a direct outcome of the dynamics of the capitalist system. Marx the historian, moreover, explicitly acknowledged his indebtedness to liberal historians. His advice to his fellow radicals was that they should "study the historical works of [the liberal historians] Thierry, Guizot, ... and others in order to enlighten themselves as to the past 'history of classes.'" Plekhanov, often called the father of Russian Marxism, repeated Marx's suggestion, noting that the liberal historians "Guizot, Minier, Augustin Thierry, and Tocqueville all recognized the predominant role of the 'economic factor,' at least in the history of the Middle Ages and of modern times."[24]

During the nineteenth century, liberal historians such as Guizot had taken great satisfaction in charting the decline of the nobility and the rise of the bourgeoisie—carrier of the values of modern civilization—from its origins in the walled cities of the late Middle Ages to their own day. Marx thought of himself as completing the research of his bourgeois predecessors when he added what they wished to ignore, the new class struggle that was supplanting the old, the proletariat versus the bourgeoisie rather than the bourgeoisie versus the nobility. "No credit is due to me," Marx told one of his comrades, "for discovering the existence of classes in modern society or the struggle between them. Long before me bourgeois historians had described the historical development of this class struggle and bourgeois economists the economic anatomy of the classes."[25]

Still, Sartre's short shrift of liberalism did in some ways mimic Marx. For however much Marx denounced the liberal defenders of the status quo, he nevertheless spent much more time, passion, and energy arguing with fellow revolutionaries, especially the anarchists. Initially he fought with the followers of Proudhon over the direction of the First International, then with Bakunin and his admirers who wished to take over the movement. After Marx, other Marxists would continue, decade in and decade out, to battle with the anarchists. Indeed, the entire history of Marxism is a record of struggles with anarchists or with various heirs of the anarchists who called themselves the true Marxists. As late as May, 1968, Sartre could stroll through the streets of Paris surrounded by both black and red flags.

Throughout his life Sartre the revolutionary was asked, in effect, to choose between contending camps of revolutionaries, the anarchists or the Marxists. His various historical writings may be seen as an ongoing effort by a committed leftist to explore the sharply competing versions of revolutionary engagement represented by anarchists and Marxists, past and present, and to resolve his ambivalence on the basis of an ever more extensive knowledge of the history of revolutionary politics. Quite naturally, against the backdrop of his preoccupation with the feuds between the anarchist and Marxist members of the revolutionary family, liberalism and its history were the least of his worries.

Interlude: Red Flags or Black?

Despite the wealth of the secondary literature on Sartre, no one has offered more than passing remarks about his stand in the battle between Marxists and anarchists for the soul of the revolutionary movement. It is best, therefore, that we offer a synopsis of the long standing debate between bearers of the red and black flags before addressing the question of where Sartre positioned himself and his historical writings in the tradition of anti-traditional, revolutionary discourse.[26]

*   *   *

Polemical exchanges between Marxists and anarchists have always fallen into the same pattern. Marxists adhere to the position that the antipathy of anarchists to leadership and disciplined organization renders effective action impossible, makes defeat inevitable, and leads to frustrated anarchists committing random acts of violence that discredit the revolutionary cause while strengthening the stranglehold of the oppressive State apparatus. Anarchists respond with the claim that an authoritarian revolutionary organization cannot possibly give birth to a libertarian society; the revolutionary organization must "prefigure" the world that will exist after victory—otherwise the revolutionary means will defeat the ends of revolution.

Between the founding of the International Working Men's Association in 1864 and its demise in 1876, Mikhail Bakunin made all the arguments against Marxist political organization that were destined to be constantly repeated throughout the long struggle between Marxists and anarchists. The French delegation, consisting of acolytes of the late Pierre-Joseph Proudhon, was highly receptive to Bakunin's message. Hating Germany as an authoritarian nation, both Proudhon and Bakunin did their best to use Marx's nationality against him, Proudhon by likening him to Luther, Bakunin by comparing him to Bismarck.[27]

"How can you expect an egalitarian and a free society to emerge from an authoritarian organization?" asked Bakunin. "The International, embryo of future human society, must be from this moment the faithful image of our principles of liberty and federation."[28] Opposed to leadership emanating from the General Council, Bakunin aimed to dissolve the International into autonomous sections, loosely federated. Like other anarchists, he believed organizations should be voluntary, temporary, invented overnight to achieve a specific objective, and then quickly disbanded. Well in advance of the advent of Leninism, Bakunin repudiated the party conceived as the vanguard of the proletariat with these words: "the organization of the forces of the proletariat ... must be the task of the proletariat itself."[29]

Marx, however, was not Lenin, and Bakunin's account of the danger emanating from Marx's leadership of the First International was as misleading as it was prophetic in the case of Lenin's Third International. Whatever resemblance to Lenin one might attribute in retrospect to Marx should be limited to March of 1850, when he spoke in favor of a seizure of power by the German socialists despite the small number of proletarians and the economically underdeveloped state of Germany; but by September 15 of that same year, he had decisively reversed his position, arguing against those who held that revolution could be based on "a mere effort of will" rather than on historically developed "material" circumstances. Not for decades, he warned, would Germany be ripe for revolution.[30]

Marx's speech of September 1850 became the position he would adhere to for the rest of his life,[31] as when he founded the First International in 1864 and then struggled to save it from Bakunin. The hot-blooded revolutionary Marx of fourteen years past, the man who in March of 1850 advocated secretive organizations, had disappeared, replaced by an older Marx who believed in "complete publicity." Under the current conditions of rapidly maturing capitalism in Europe, affirmed Marx, "all sects are essentially reactionary."[32]

Waiting for circumstances to ripen rather than seeking revolution through a foolish act of will—the lesson Marx drew in September 1850—later became a standard theme in Marxian polemics against anarchists. "Historical conditions" versus "will" separated Marx from Bakunin and the anarchists who knew little history, cared less, and simply rose up whenever the opportunity presented itself, no matter how hopeless the outcome. "Spontaneity" was the magical word of Bakunin and other anarchists: whenever the moment felt right, Bakunin would strike. To him, the Paris Commune of 1871 was rooted in "the spontaneous and continued action of the masses," admirably so, because the only alternative he could envision was dictatorship under "authoritarian communists."[33]

Of all Marxists, the one who repudiated "spontaneity" most vigorously was Lenin. "Subservience to spontaneity," he wrote in *What Is to Be Done?*, was what was responsible for the irresponsible violence of the anarchist terrorists and the irresponsible compromise mongering of their opposites in the socialist movement, the "Economists," who followed the labor movement instead of leading it. "The spontaneous working-class movement is by itself able to create ... only trade unionism, and working class trade-unionist politics is precisely working-class bourgeois politics." As a result of their capitulation to spontaneity, the Economists stand at the tail rather than the head of the movement, "gazing with awe ... upon the 'posterior' of the Russian proletariat."[34]

To hear Lenin denounce "spontaneity," one might believe he was the most orthodox of Marxists when in truth his position in the "will" versus "conditions" debate proves just the opposite. No less than the anarchists, he stressed the will because there was no point in waiting. At most, historical conditions will give rise to trade-union consciousness, never to revolutionary consciousness. Therefore his vanguard elite must make the revolution for the workers, despite the workers, whenever and wherever an opportunity arises, even in a backward country. Intolerant of revisionists, Lenin himself was in fact the most revisionist of Marxists.

On only one matter, the will, and only by accident, did Lenin have anything in common with the anarchists he despised. There were, however, other Marxists who drank deeply from the well of anarchism. As of 1896, the anarchists were tossed out of the Second International, with the result that revolutionaries harboring anarchist sentiments frequently stayed within the movement by injecting their beliefs into the body of officially Marxist thought. Hybrid figures who labeled themselves Marxists but were really anarcho-Marxists came to the fore, usually for the sake of beseeching an established, stodgy, or authoritarian Marxism to return to its original libertarian message.

One such memorable figure was Rosa Luxemburg, who challenged Lenin's conception of a hierarchical and centralized party, organized in imitation of an army, and staffed with professional revolutionaries. When Rosa questioned Lenin, first in 1904 and then shortly after the Russian Revolution, the revolutionaries had to admit that she was ideally qualified to confront the leader of the Bolsheviks. Like Lenin, she came to reject Karl Kautsky, leader of the Second International (1889–1916), because his politics was revolutionary in rhetoric but incrementalist in substance. Her disdain for "parliamentary cretinism" and the reformism of trade unions was matched only by Lenin's. And yet she was as supportive of the anarchist themes of "spontaneity" and the need of the workers to liberate themselves as Lenin was hostile to the same in *What Is to Be Done?* (1902) and *One Step Forward, Two Steps Back* (1904). Writing against Lenin in 1904, she argued that "the errors committed by a truly revolutionary movement are infinitely more fruitful than the infallibility of the cleverest Central Committee." All the great Russian events of the preceding ten years—the general strikes of 1896 and 1903, the street demonstrations of 1901—were "the spontaneous product of the movement in ferment." No anarchist could have said it better.[35]

Rosa Luxemburg attacked Lenin again after his emergence in late 1917 as the leader of a revolutionary government. She began with several gestures reaffirming her credentials as an arch-radical, most notably by decrying Kautsky's Second International and crediting the November Revolution with salvaging the honor of international socialism. Then she proceeded to register her disappointment that the Bolshevik version of the "dictatorship of the proletariat" was not in the least a regime run by the workers; rather, it was "a dictatorship in the bourgeois sense, in the sense of the rule of the Jacobins." Much was wrong with parliamentary democracy, yet "the remedy which Trotsky and Lenin have found, the elimination of democracy, is worse than the disease it is supposed to cure." True socialist democracy "is not something which begins only in the promised land after the foundations of the socialist economy are created.... It begins at the very moment of the seizure of power.... It is the same thing as the dictatorship of the proletariat."[36]

* * *

Marx's speeches of March and September, 1850, were made so early in his career that he was not yet Marx, not yet a mature and highly influential figure in left-wing politics; nevertheless, each of his two contrasting statements in 1850 was pregnant with a distinctive version of future Marxist revolutionary strategy: the speech of September presaged Kautsky and the Second International; the speech of March, Lenin and the Third.

Head of the Second International, intellectual mentor of Russian Marxists, Karl Kautsky was horrified when Trotsky and Lenin seized power in Russia. To his mind, taking power in a backward country could only mean a repeat of Robespierre or Napoleon. In the unlikely event that Lenin's regime proved lasting, Bolshevism might be the victor but socialism would surely lose; for then the Russian so-called "dictatorship of the proletariat" would be more accurately termed "Asiatic" or "Tartar socialism."[37] To fend off the charge of "renegade" that Lenin hurled at him,[38] Kautsky pointed out that Marx in September of 1850 had permanently broken with the position he had taken in March. The revolution must be based on mature conditions, not on will. The Bolsheviks, in their attempt to impose change overnight by a pure act of will, resembled "the Bakunists of Spain in the year 1873."[39]

Trotsky refuted Kautsky and other Marxists guilty of rejecting the Bolshevik takeover by citing the Marx of March 1850, who had ended his speech with a battle cry for "permanent revolution." To Marx in the early months of 1850, to Trotsky in the early twentieth century, "permanent revolution" meant combining two revolutions into one by taking whatever steps were necessary to ensure that what begins as a bourgeois revolution will very quickly end with the proletariat in power, actively cajoling the workers of other countries to follow its example. If revolution in Russia sparked an uprising in highly developed Germany, all would be well.[40]

Anarchists had a very different understanding of permanent revolution. Usually it meant to them that no society should ever be permitted to settle down into an institutionalized routine stifling the "spontaneity" of its members. Even Proudhon, many of whose sentiments leaned in a conservative direction, sprinkled his writings with paeans to spontaneity and maintained that "in history there is permanent revolution and, strictly speaking, there have not been several revolutions, but only one and the same permanent revolution."[41] In its most full-blooded manifestation, permanent revolution to an anarchist entails the reinvention of society day after day, endlessly.

Such was Sartre's revolutionary inheritance. The question now becomes, what did he make of it?

Sartre's Leftist Itinerary

All through his life, Sartre was a man leaning toward the left, from early manhood to old age, including the days of his youth when both his lifestyle and his emerging philosophy might lead us to expect him to be apolitical. But what kind of leftist would he be? The story of his flirtations, now with one left and then with another, the tale of his ongoing ideological experimentation, is complex, tangled, and perhaps confusing. Here we do not pretend to recount his every move; our goal is not to recite every chapter of the story. Rather, our more modest objective is to provide whatever backstory is necessary to appreciate his efforts when writing history to resolve his ideological dilemmas and pursue his political agendas.

Before the war, recollected Simone de Beauvoir, the intellectual "we had admired the most" was Alain, whose habit of "saying No" had been "the hallmark of our generation."[42] Endlessly Alain rose in protest against the established authorities, the bureaucrats, the city of Paris, the elites, the elected officials, and in favor of the people; his message was ever one of protest and rebellion.[43] It is telling that Camus, author of *The Rebel*, admired "this 'everyday courage' of which Alain spoke,"[44] and equally telling that the mature Sartre, for all his admiration of those who "said No" to the Nazis and other oppressors, had absolutely no use for Alain, a figure whose rebellion always stopped well short of revolution and socialism.

Alain, situated on the fringes of a party that called itself "Radical," was enamored of the old France and dedicated to a politics of restoration. That was enough to make him a figure of no interest to Sartre as World War II ended and the time had come to construct a new France. In his notebooks of the late 1940s, Sartre blamed Alain for his ahistorical outlook and his frozen, Stoic morality[45]—attitudes that Sartre was busy purging from his own thought (see Chapter 3).

Already in the 1930s, as Simone de Beauvoir's account makes clear, Sartre was little tempted by any radicalism that was not radical. In 1931, she recalled, "our anarchism was as deep-dyed and aggressive as that of the old libertarians.… We were against institutionalism, which seemed incompatible with freedom, and likewise opposed to the bourgeoisie." During those early years "our love of freedom, our opposition to the established order of things, our individualism, and our respect for the working classes—all these brought us close to the anarchist position" but, she was quick to add, "our incoherence defied any sort of label."[46]

What fed their "antibourgeois anarchism" was their hatred of anything "normal" and love of everything "extreme." Fashionable people, Sunday crowds, children, families, and "any sort of humanism" they loathed, de Beauvoir reminisced; anything monstrous they embraced, which explains their fascination with what André Breton termed the "indestructible kernel of darkness" lurking in everyone. They despised the parliamentary Socialist party because "reformism was repugnant to our temperaments: society could only change globally, in one fell swoop, by a violent convulsion."[47]

On a number of occasions in de Beauvoir's memoirs of the early years the topic of "permanent revolution" comes to the fore, usually in its anarchist meaning of a revolution every day. Sometimes she applied the term "permanent revolution" to the personal lives of herself and Sartre, as when she wrote, "we created our own attitudes, theories, ideas, though we refused to be chained to them, preferring to practice permanent revolution." At other times, she and Sartre pondered the directly political meaning of this famous expression: "We had the very highest opinion of Trotsky, and the idea of 'permanent revolution' suited our anarchist tendencies." All the foregoing was based, she noted, on their reading of such anarcho-Marxists as Rosa Luxemburg and the Trotsky of "the revolution betrayed," whom anarcho-Marxists adopted, however misleadingly, as one of their own.[48]

To all appearances, identification with anarchism initially came naturally, almost unreflectively, to de Beauvoir and Sartre because it matched perfectly their bohemian lifestyle. With the passage of time, there is evidence, however, that they began to address anarchism more seriously and quite critically under the pressure of events, most notably the Spanish Civil War. They blamed the anarchists in Spain for refusing to acknowledge that "before making a revolution they had to win the war." Lack of unity and unwillingness to take orders "constituted the most frightful danger, especially when dealing with Franco's homogeneous army." Establishing local soviets was the obsession of the anarchists at a time when their concern should have been to "boost output in the factories." Anarchist-Syndicalist insurrection, anarchist and Trotskyist outbreaks, played directly into the hands of the Fascists, thought de Beauvoir and Sartre.[49]

So their anarchism had its limits, and it is noteworthy that all through the 1930s they flirted with the alternative revolutionary commitment, Communism. "We got to asking ourselves whether it was enough for us to sympathize with the struggle being fought by the working classes," de Beauvoir remembered. "Ought we not to join it? More than once during these years Sartre was vaguely tempted to join the Communist Party." Although they feared that membership would conflict with their calling as writers, they could not help but admire the strong organization that enabled Communists to pursue their objectives successfully.

More than anything else, that which made it impossible for them to seek membership was the Molotov-Ribbentrop Pact of 1939: "Though we had plenty of reservations about the goings-on inside the U.S.S.R, we nevertheless had believed hitherto that the Soviet Government served the cause of world revolution. This treaty proved, in the most brutal way, that … the Trotskyites and every left-wing opposition group were right after all,"[50] remarked de Beauvoir on behalf of both herself and Sartre.

It is clear that despite the apolitical message of *Nausea*, Sartre was strongly interested in Communist politics by the mid-1930s. "Apolitical, stubbornly refusing any commitment, my heart, of course, was with the Left,"[51] Sartre wrote when he recalled the period during which the question was whether to join the Party or not to join. *The Transcendence of the Ego*, 1936, proves that at a very early stage in his philosophical career he was interested in the theory no less than the practice of Marxism. Near the end of his phenomenological treatise, he remarked that "it has always seemed to me that a working hypothesis as fruitful as historical materialism never needed for a foundation the absurdity which is metaphysical materialism."[52] While writing about Husserl, Sartre set forth a decade in advance the view he would elaborate in his essay of 1946 on "Materialism and Revolution"—Marxism, yes, but not the vulgar, deterministic Marxism of the Communist Party.

No doubt it was his schoolboy friendship with Paul Nizan that forced Sartre to think and rethink his stand on Marxism. Their interactions at the Lycée Henri IV made it impossible for Sartre simply to walk away from the Marxism that Nizan championed. As late as 1960, Sartre wrote a lengthy essay mostly in praise in Nizan,[53] who had died at Dunkerque; and one may find in *Roads to Freedom,* Sartre's multivolume postwar novel, a continuing dialogue between Sartre and Nizan in the characters of Mathieu, the existentialist in all but name, and Brunet, the committed Communist.

Where, then, did Sartre stand in the battles between anarchists and Marxists when he embarked on his historical writings? Had he abandoned the anarchist outlook, which was his at the beginning? Several remarks in *What Is Literature?* (1947) offer valuable clues. First of all, there is a passage in which he articulated a view that inevitably brings to mind the anarchist understanding of "permanent revolution." Boldly he called for a society not only "without classes" but also "without stability." One must write for "a public which has the freedom of changing everything; which means … constant renewal of frameworks, and the continuous overthrowing of order once it tends to congeal. In short, literature is the subjectivity of a society in permanent revolution."[54] This was anarchism pure and simple, a political extension, arguably, of his remark in 1936 that "each instant of our conscious life reveals to us a creation *ex nihilo.*"[55] Or, better yet, it was a collectivization of the lessons taught in *Being and Nothingness*: individuals, as understood in that famous philosophical treatise, faced the burden each day of choosing who they would be; now it was the entire society that was to make the same choice, day in and day out, permanently.

A second passage in *What Is Literature?,* or a series of interrelated passages, concerns what Sartre dubbed "Trotskyising Surrealism." It was André Breton's style of anarchism that Sartre had in mind, the Surrealist movement that in the 1930s rejected Stalin by endorsing the Trotsky of "the revolution betrayed." After Breton and the Surrealists have grown tired of their reign of highly cultured destruction, what emerges from the wreckage is not, for all their pretenses, Trotsky's program, but instead "a Nothingness which is only the endless fluttering of contradictions." Theirs is a futile endeavor, Sartre complained, to "leap out of the human condition." The Surrealist obsession with violence lends their writings a "disturbing resemblance to the political writings of Charles Maurras." When discussing Surrealism in *What Is Literature?,* Sartre condemned anarchism as vehemently as he praised it when issuing his own call for permanent revolution in the same text.[56]

A third passage in *What Is Literature?* is especially noteworthy for our purposes because in it, Sartre spelled out his view of the proper relationship between anarchism and Marxism. What he wanted was a Marxism that "would have had to absorb rival doctrines, digest them, and remain open." Unfortunately, the history of the First International is that of Marx's victory and Proudhon's defeat. "It would take a long time," remarked Sartre, "to tell all that this triumph without glory has cost Marxism; for want of contradiction, it has lost life." Marxism benefitted whenever it was forced to "steal its enemies' arms"; left unchallenged on the Left, "it became the Church."[57]

Sartre's comments in 1947 on the need for an anarchist challenge to a Marxist status quo set the stage for the seemingly contradictory remarks he uttered much later. In 1969, he wrote "It is obvious that anarchism leads nowhere, today as yesterday."[58] But that did not prevent him from remarking in 1968 that "I have always remained an anarchist" or from taking the stance in 1975 that "I have always thought that anarchy … must be brought about." Sartre, in his distinctive fashion, belonged to the anarcho-Marxist tradition, which injected its anarchism without acknowledgment into the body of Marxism, and included such diverse figures as Rosa Luxemburg, the "left-wing Communists" against whom Lenin fulminated in 1920, Georges Sorel and his version of Syndicalism, some of the Surrealists, and many of the students of May '68. No matter how far Sartre moved in the direction of Marxist analysis, his anarchism never completely disappeared. What was he conjuring up in 1975 if not anarchism when he called for "libertarian socialism" and "the rejection of all hierarchies—the rejection of the very notion of a leader"?[59]

Over the years, many nominal Marxists have carefully hidden their anarchist souls from public view, the better to situate themselves so that they might restore an established Marxism to its libertarian roots. Sartre's case was more complicated. Back and forth he moved between the two revolutionary commitments, always ready to borrow from one or the other as circumstances demanded, putting both to a series of tests through his studies of history. Disdaining a set of predetermined, ideologically dictated answers, Sartre chose to become a committed and studious historian of revolution.

Sartre, Historian of Revolution

Taking a stand on the French and Russian revolutions was the price of admission to the revolutionary movement—the proof of belonging for intellectuals on the left. No one, then, should be surprised to learn that the accomplished philosopher Jean-Paul Sartre toyed from 1947 to 1952 with the idea of writing biographies of the deputies of the French Constituent Assembly, 1789–1791, or that he considered writing a biography of Robespierre.[60] Nor, presumably, should anyone have been taken aback, when it finally appeared in 1985, to discover that Sartre devoted almost half the pages of his unfinished second volume of the *Critique of Dialectical Reason* to the history of events related to the Russian Revolution.

André Breton voiced one anarchist possibility when he proclaimed that "when it comes to revolt, none of us must have any need of ancestors."[61] Far more typical, however, was Kropotkin's anarchist history of *The Great French Revolution* or the historical chapter Daniel Cohn-Bendit wrote in 1968 on "The Strategy and Nature of Bolshevism" for his *Senile Communism: The Left-Wing Alternative,* which was an anarchist assault on Lenin's *Left Wing Communism: An Infantile Disorder.* For Breton's boast that that "we combat … scholarly research,"[62] Sartre had nothing but contempt. Willingness to engage in painstaking studies of the history of revolution Sartre was convinced, as were many anarchists and all Marxists, was an inescapable component of revolutionary commitment.

In the first volume of the *Critique of Dialectical Reason* (1960) Sartre aimed "to explain the transition of oppressed classes … to the state of revolutionary group *praxis.*"[63] In the second volume a central concern was to offer an expansive account of the struggles between Trotsky and Stalin. Although the two volumes of the *Critique* were his most ambitious, albeit unfinished, treatment of revolutionary history, he wrote constantly on related topics throughout the 1950s. Usually, as in *The Communists and Peace* (1952–1954) or *The Ghost of Stalin* (1956–1957), he directed his efforts toward an event in contemporary France or Russia, striving to place an immediate problem in a larger historical perspective. Whether out in the open or just underneath the surface, in all of these writings—from the most journalistic to the most philosophical—he constantly took up the old battles between Marxists and anarchists.

Much of what Sartre sought in his historical writings was to check the anarchistic impulses of his youth. We have previously examined his historical account in *The Communists and Peace* of the transformation of the French working force from skilled to unskilled, from a proletariat armed with proud traditions to one denied the comfort of having a history (see Chapter 3). Here we must add that he displayed precious little sympathy for the skilled workers of times past, who gathered together under the banner of anarcho-Syndicalism. Instead, his history reads as a debunking of the union democracy of "the good old days." Which democracy he asked? "The only one ever practiced was aristocratic."[64] Against the anarchists of his own day, enemies of the discipline of the Communist party, he pointed out what had lain underneath the Syndicalist leader Fernand Pelloutier's

Bergsonian cult of "spontaneous and creative action": "the *élan vital* of the working classes concealed the dictatorship of the skilled elite."[65] So-called revolutionary Syndicalism was biased in favor of a workers' elite and dishonest in its refusal to admit that such victories as it had enjoyed were the result of strong leadership.

It followed that no Syndicalist of Sartre's day had a right to criticize the French Communist party for attempting to impose discipline upon the workers. Hence Sartre penned an impassioned attack on Claude Lefort's anarchist-inspired repudiation of *The Communists and Peace,* no matter that both men wrote for *Les Temps Modernes.*[66] Lefort criticized and Sartre applauded the efforts of the Communists to transform the workers who had been reduced to passive, atomized "masses" into newly organized, active "classes." Enamored of anarcho-Syndicalism, Lefort falsely maintained—in Sartre's words—that "the proletariat is in essence revolutionary" and need only follow its "spontaneous" impulses to be successful.[67] Unfortunately, nothing could be further from the truth.

No matter how far Sartre's thought evolved after the early 1950s, it is noteworthy that he renewed the demystification of Syndicalist anarchism in *Critique of Dialectical Reason* that he had initiated in *The Communists and Peace.* The same historical presentation of the Syndicalists, the same revolutionary downgrading of their achievements, may be found in 1960 as in 1952.[68]

Repeatedly cutting one's ties with the historical record of anarchism in its Syndicalist guise is, however, not necessarily a rejection of all forms of anarchism. In other passages of the *Critique,* Sartre wrote that "the [so-called] 'wretched of the earth' are precisely the only people capable of changing life, and who do change it every day."[69] The similarity to Bakunin is striking. "To me," Bakunin had asserted, "the flower of the proletariat is not, as it is to the Marxists, the upper layer, the aristocracy of labor." As would be true for Fanon and Sartre at a later date, Bakunin was convinced that the revolution would arise from the ranks of "the uncultivated, the disinherited, the miserable, the illiterates."[70]

Sartre's position parallels Bakunin's but parallel lines never intersect. Bakunin's was a romantic fixation on outlaws and outsiders; much the same was de Beauvoir's admission that in her youth "I was attracted by those people, such as madmen, prostitutes, or tramps, who had in one way or another denied their own humanity."[71] Sartre, the mature thinker, in direct contrast, was out to show how tough-minded he was, how realist. Each time he looked to "subhumans" to rise up against their "betters," he did so while abjuring all romantic fascination with outsiders. Despite the similarities, Sartre was different from Bakunin, the difference taking the form of Bakunin's eulogy of "spontaneity" as the source of revolution and Sartre's denial of the same.

Neither Sartre the philosopher nor Sartre the politician/historian responded affirmatively to the anarchist eulogy of spontaneity. So far as the philosopher was concerned, the anarchist claim that spontaneity was the source of social uprisings reeked of the false claim, which Sartre had disposed of early in his career, that individuals act admirably when they capitulate to emotion. Just as each person, according to Sartre, must assume the burden of organizing his or her life, so must the members of a revolutionary social movement rise above themselves, rationally calculating their strategy and tactics rather than acting on momentary impulse.

Sartre the politician and historian likewise posited the finding that revolution had not been and could not be based on spontaneity. It was while discussing the historical record of the French left in *The Communists and Peace* that Sartre initiated what would prove to be a series of relentless attacks upon "spontaneity." Sartre began by complaining that the appeal to spontaneity is really a call for a given "essence" of the workers to assert itself, which "amounts to subordinating doing to being, action to passion." The worker "escapes the harsh necessity of unifying what he thinks, what he feels, and what he does." His unity is given in advance so he need not "make himself." Worse, "organization stifles the free élan of the heart, therefore, *true* spontaneity can not stand being organized." In the anarchist universe, leaders are told "you must limit yourself to deciphering the messages flowing from the revolutionary instinct of the workers."[72]

In *The Communists and Peace,* Sartre's argument was that the revolution is bound to fail if left to those who count on "spontaneity" to do the hard work of organization. A truly revolutionary movement "can be conceived of only as an *authority.* It is anything but the delightful product of the workers' spontaneity: it imposes itself on each *individual* as an imperative." Explicitly citing Lenin's *What Is to Be Done?,* Sartre took the position that "the Party represents for each one the most austere ethic: it is a matter of entering a new life by casting off one's present personality....Without it, there is no unity, no action, no class."[73]

Four years later, Sartre wrote *The Ghost of Stalin* in response to the Russian invasion of Hungary. While he had deep misgivings about the actions of the Soviet leadership, he saw no reason why the uprisings in Hungary should alter his view of "spontaneity." What happened in the streets was not a matter of spontaneity but of unification of the many by the party against the party.[74] In the most general sense, Sartre announced, "it is not spontaneity that pushes the masses to armed insurrection, it is need."[75] Need now, as ever, is what compels the masses to act together; action is a response to external pressure, not an upsurge of an internal essence. In the *Critique of Dialectical Reason,* Sartre would cite need as the driving force of history.

"Ultrabolshevism" was the label Merleau-Ponty in 1955 pinned on *The Communists and Peace.*[76] Sartre refrained from launching a counterattack on the old friend who had introduced him to Marxist modes of thought. Had he answered, Sartre might well have said that Bolshevism is required in some instances but not in others, depending on historical circumstances. If in Hungary, 1956, the party wrongly assumed it was to make all the decisions for the workers, that was because the regime had fallen out of touch with history; the time for de-Stalinization had arrived, but the party was not equal to the task. The de-Stalinizers had forgotten to de-Stalinize themselves. Earlier, supposedly at his most "Bolshevik" in *The Communists and Peace,* Sartre had carefully refrained from limiting the French proletariat to a passive acceptance of the Party's dictates: "I wish only to show that class unity can be neither passively received nor spontaneously produced." His point was that from the moment the proletariat has been united, even if it required the party to do the uniting, it "can go beyond its leaders, steer them farther than they meant to go and can translate into the *social* sphere an initial decision which was perhaps only *political.*"[77] Once shaped and molded by the party, the French proletariat can come to life and assume control of its destiny.

At stake here was the old question of "will" versus "historical conditions" in revolutionary debates. The more Sartre advanced in historical knowledge, the less he could continue issuing an anarchist call, as he had in *What Is Literature?,* for revolution here and now, followed by another revolution every day, as a succession of pure acts of will. Equally unacceptable was the version of Marxism based on the assumption that ripe historical conditions will make the revolution for us. Finally, although the Leninist "will" to revolution through the agency of the vanguard party in a backward country might sometimes be the most promising beginning, it should never be permitted to degenerate into end as well as means. Sartre's historical writings aimed to throw on the rubbish heap all these old debates: will versus circumstances; anarchist will versus Leninist will.

To make his case, Sartre in *Critique of Dialectical Reason* cited evidence drawn from the French Revolution. At the outset, he noted that it is common "to contrast a centralizing, authoritarian tendency coming *from above* ... with a democratic, spontaneous tendency which grows from the base.... They are treated as two *essentially* opposed realities, only the second of which can really constitute the group as common self-creation." Such a contrast, he affirms, is utterly untenable. Historians of the French Revolution have long drawn our attention to popular agitators around whom "the organization would form in moments of tension" but who did not issue orders: "It would be absurd to use them as an argument against the democracy of the popular organization." Even the movement toward violence was a matter of "*fraternity-terror,*" both top-down and bottom-up. Daniel Guérin's well-known 1946 anarchist history of the French Revolution is wrong; the very idea of having to choose between revolution "from above" and "from below" is wrong. The best way to begin a history of the French or any revolution is to realize that "this is not and cannot be an issue about … Lenin, Rosa Luxemburg, Stalin, or Trotsky."[78] The best histories will be written by those who seek to transcend the old anarchist/Marxist antinomy.

Fully a decade before publication of the first volume of the *Critique*, Sartre had set the stage for his mature work while reviewing a book on Tito's breakaway Communist Yugoslavia. Sartre in 1950 was pleased that the Yugoslav socialists, acting independently of the Kremlin, were helping militant Communists discover the significance of "subjective factors" in history and that their experiment raised the hope that an "infallible bureaucracy" would be countered by "perpetual autocritique." It disturbed him, however, that the Yugoslav spokespersons often sounded like Rosa Luxemburg, who had failed to understand that the Marxism she imbibed "at the breast of Imperial Germany was indefensible in 1917 in Soviet Russia," and who employed an unfortunate rhetoric of immediacy and "spontaneity."[79]

Asked late in life to draw lessons from his mature historical writings, Sartre announced that "the dilemma spontaneity/party is a false problem." All his efforts in the *Critique* had aimed to show that "a fused group … is born in the stress of a particular situation and not because of some kind of 'spontaneity.'" Sometimes "the mass, by itself, does not possess *spontaneity*" and requires leadership; by no means, however, should the workers, the oppressed, the wretched of the earth, follow the party blindly and forever. They must, at the proper moment, reassert their "sovereignty" because the party will in the natural course of its evolution become "a closed, static system, which has a tendency to sclerosis." Sartre's final verdict was that a proper revolution has, so to speak, both its Leninist and its anarchist moments.[80]

*   *   *

Whether Sartre in his historical writings forged his own brand of anarcho-Marxism or transcended the old quarrels between Marxists and anarchists is open to debate. What cannot be questioned is the ferocity with which he repudiated the anarcho-Marxism of other intellectuals, Rosa Luxemburg for one; but most of all, he never tired of chastising anarcho-Marxists who hid under the name of Trotskyist. His ultimate refutation, arguably, came in the second volume of the *Critique of Dialectical Reason,* where he settled old revolutionary scores in the course of writing a history of the conflict between Trotsky and Stalin.

That anyone of anarchist sympathies should look to Trotsky for an icon was obviously not without its ironies. Who more than Trotsky was willing to use the Red Army to crush the forces of anarchism during the early years of the Russian Revolution? Some bearers of the black flag in later years, such as Daniel Cohn-Bendit in 1968, did express dissatisfaction with Trotsky,[81] but it is remarkable how often intellectuals and activists who were anarchists in all but official title—enemies of Stalin and mourners for "the revolution betrayed"—rallied to the banner of Trotsky. Anarchists had hidden under Marxist labels after being threatened with expulsion from the Second International; anarchists did the same years later when coming to terms with the Third International, and sought to turn Trotsky's conflict with Stalin to their polemical advantage.

Year after year, Sartre fought with Trotskyists. For example, his aggressive attack on Claude Lefort in 1953 was directed at a thinker who, Sartre believed, was an anarchist masquerading as a follower of Trotsky. As early as 1948, Sartre and the editorial board of *Les Temps Modernes* had complained that "for Lefort, the U.S.S.R. is the *accused.* For us, with its grandeurs and its horrors, it is an enterprise which has [temporarily] broken down."[82]

Of all the Trotskyists, the ones whom Sartre hated most were the Surrealists, objects of his contempt in *What Is Literature?* and a constant source of derision throughout his later career. Never could he see in Breton and his cohort anything more than exhibitionists who did more to harm than serve the revolutionary cause. Even at his most violent, Sartre could not have written, as did Breton, that "the simplest Surrealist act consists of dashing down into the street, pistol in hand, and firing blindly, as fast as you can pull the trigger, into the crowd."[83] Underneath the shock tactics of the Surrealists, Sartre spied a pampered group of artists who "leave everything in place," whose "revolutionary doctrines remain purely theoretical," and who "remain the parasites of the social class they insult."[84]

The Surrealist Trotskyists were easy targets but what of Trotsky himself? During the immediate postwar years, when he was still trying to steer a middle course between the American and Russian camps, Sartre was more attentive to "Trotskyising Surrealists" than to Trotsky.[85] Once Sartre chose the Communist side in the early 1950s, it became increasingly difficult for him to remain silent on Trotsky. At first he handled the issue by making a distinction between Trotskyists of all stripes—not just the Surrealists—and Trotsky. Those who enlisted under Trotsky's banner he chided because they foolishly invoked a "revolutionary instinct" on the part of the workers and failed to search historically for the "external factors" that are the necessary preparation for a major upheaval. Not so Trotsky himself: "his conception," Sartre pointed out to a Trotskyist, "remains much richer and more complex than yours." He quoted in *The Communists and Peace* from *The Revolution Betrayed* and *The Permanent Revolution* to prove that Trotsky was far from being a Trotskyist. It was party leadership on which Trotsky counted, not "the essence-in-movement of the proletariat."[86]

The second volume of the *Critique of Dialectical Reason* was a culminating moment in that Sartre no longer separated the unworthy Trotskyists from the man they claimed as their leader. Instead, he dared undertake the project of demystifying Trotsky himself. He would do so while writing a history of the conflict between Trotsky and Stalin that supposedly bracketed moral judgment and featured neither a demon nor a saint, limiting himself strictly to telling a story of actions and consequences, failure and success. Whereas Trotsky's very brilliance was his shortcoming as a revolutionary in Sartre's account, Stalin's dull, plodding person figured in the second volume of the *Critique* as the salvation of the Russian Revolution. Here, as elsewhere, irony figures prominently in "dialectical reason," as employed by Sartre.[87]

The backdrop, Sartre insists, for understanding the conflict between Trotsky and Stalin—Trotsky's "permanent revolution" versus Stalin's "socialism in one country"—was that "Russia's relationship with Western Europe" had been lived historically "as a gigantic mediation between Asia and Europe, … a perpetually contested synthesis of European and Asiatic populations." The more immediate problem was that in Russia "the proletariat represented practically nothing, while the [backward] rural masses constituted virtually the totality of the population." Under such exceptionally difficult circumstances, the revolution could only survive by means of deferring international revolution and accepting "the ideological monstrosity of 'socialism in one country.'" To swallow such a bitter pill in our own time is not a matter of becoming a Stalinist; it is, Sartre asserted, merely to learn the lessons of history: "It is strictly an example and we shall not consider it *for its own sake* but for its educational value."[88]

What Sartre learned from the struggle between Trotsky and Stalin was that revolutionary ideology should never be permitted to undermine the revolutionary cause. Trotsky was "first and foremost a theoretician, an intellectual. In action he remained an intellectual, which meant action had to be *radical*. Such a structure of practice is perfectly valid provided it is adapted to circumstances, which is what allowed him to organize the Army and win the war." Eventually, however, Trotsky's "abstract" and "universal" ideology prevented him from serving Soviet Russia wisely. Stalin could not respect Trotsky's left-wing argument for rapid, forced industrialization, since it was ideology, not an examination of Russian circumstances, that dictated Trotsky's stand. Nor was there anything to be said for the right wing's "socialism at a snail's pace," which "likewise struck Stalin as purely theoreticist," being based not on practical realities but on "general considerations regarding underdeveloped countries."[89]

Stalin alone understood Russia, not intellectually perhaps, but intimately if inarticulately in the core of his uncultured, brutal being. Unlike other major Russian Marxists, he had never been an *émigré* and knew precious little about the Western Europe of which Marx spoke. Trotskyists, by contrast, were "Westerners," out to impose a Western ideology upon Russia, where it fit so poorly. Exiled, Trotsky "rediscovered via Trotskyism the abstract universality of Marxism." Trotskyism, rather than attempting to understand Russia, charged Sartre, "represented revolutionary Europe striving to release itself from the Soviet grip." Whereas Trotskyism was abstract and ahistorical, Stalinism was "*historical* and singular." To be faithful to the Revolution, Sartre was convinced, one had to come to terms with "the grandiose, terrible, and irreversible temporalization that in History was to take the name of *Stalinism.*"[90]

Readers long familiar with *The Ghost of Stalin* (1956–1957) found in the second volume of the *Critique of Dialectical Reason*, when it finally appeared, arguments with which they were quite familiar. Already in 1956 Sartre held that "only those who participate, in the East and the West, in the movement of socialism can and should judge."[91] Again, well in advance of the *Critique* he argued that "'Socialism in one country,' or Stalinism, does not constitute a deviation from socialism: it is the long way around which is imposed by circumstances."[92] Also in 1956, as he would later, he answered the question "Must one give the name of socialism to this bloody monster? ... I answer frankly: yes."[93] In many respects the difference between *The Ghost of Stalin* and the *Second Critique* came down to this: that what was simply alluded to in the first book was supplemented in the sequel by a significant amount of historical investigation.

Anyone who stood outside the revolutionary movement could only express dismay that Sartre was willing to excuse so many of Stalin's violent deeds in the *Second Critique,* not to mention that he simply passed over in silence numerous other of Stalin's most vile undertakings. But we must remember, of course, that the latter volume of the *Critique* was meant not for the liberals he despised but for his fellow revolutionary intellectuals, whether anarchists, Trotskyists, Marxists, or Leninists. It was also meant for himself: once and for all, to all appearances, he had buried one of his former selves, the anarchist self who in *What Is Literature?* had called for an everyday, permanent revolution.

This much must be said for Sartre: he was careful to provide himself with an escape route from his arguments on behalf of the Soviet Union. When Russia suppressed the Hungarian revolt in 1956, he was willing to criticize a socialist power on the grounds that it was failing to live up to the promise of socialism. Twelve years later, in August 1968, when Russia invaded Czechoslovakia out of fear of that country's "communism with a human face," Sartre announced that he had had enough. "Today the Soviet model is no longer valid," he declared.[94] "After the month of August 1968, it is necessary … to abandon reformist illusions about this type of regime. The machine cannot be repaired; the peoples of Eastern Europe must seize hold of it and destroy it."[95]

*   *   *

It would be a mistake to assume that the older Sartre grew and the greater his immersion in historical studies, the more he left behind the anarchist hankerings and inklings of his youth. His story is less straightforward, less predictable. By his own admission, he had been in his early days "a throwback to anarchy" and might never have moved decisively to a more satisfactory position had it not been for the intervention of Merleau-Ponty.[96] As late as 1960, on a visit to Latin America, he called on the youth of the day to inject some anarchy into Marxism.[97] Even in his most mature historical thought on revolution, one can discern what might be called an anarchist element; or, to borrow from Hegel, we might say that although anarchism is not the entirety of his later thought, it does constitute one "moment" in his account of the revolutionary process, as for example when he discussed July 14, 1789.

As youngsters, Simone de Beauvoir recalled, she and Sartre had sympathy for proletarian revolution in Russia—but only in its early stage, not for what followed.[98] As a mature thinker, Sartre did not afford himself the luxury of saying yes to one moment of revolution but no to the rest. Nevertheless, his account of the seizing of the Bastille in the *Critique of Dialectical Reason* is such that the reader readily senses that for him this famous event was a special moment in the French Revolution—a moment permitting him to indulge, if only for a moment, his old anarchist sympathies.

At the very beginning of the French Revolution, and particularly in the taking of the Bastille, Sartre saw "the nation as a totality reshaping itself, the nation as permanent revolution."[99] The anarchist overtones of his formulation are difficult to miss. Not yet encumbered by institutions, or a bureaucracy, or a ruling elite, the people of Paris heading down the street to the Bastille were a *groupe en fusion*. Individuals acted together, sought the same goals, but never lost themselves when acting in concert with others. What had been a mere "gathering" (*rassemblement*) became, without plan or foresight, a "group-in-fusion." The orders that were shouted—"to the Bastille!"—were issued by no one and everyone,[100] each person seeing himself in the other. "In [such] *praxis* there is no *Other*, there are only several myselves."[101] Admittedly, it required an external threat—the troops forming around Versailles—to spark the coalescence of a "series" of isolated individuals into a group, which perhaps means the analogy with anarchism is not perfect. Yet it is astonishing to hear Sartre, when speaking of the Parisians on July 14, 1789, voice approvingly the most anarchist of words, spontaneity: "in the spontaneous *praxis* of the group-in-fusion, free activity is realized by everyone."[102]

Anarchism is not forever, but occasionally it is a historical reality for a moment and that moment is to be treasured all the more keenly precisely because it cannot last.

An Unfinished Finale

Sartre managed to have it both ways in his later years. On the one hand, there was the Sartre who in the 1970s permitted one part of the second *Critique of Dialectical Reason* to be published, and the selection in question was none other than his sympathetic account of Stalin's ascendancy.[103] On the other hand, there was the Sartre who was enabled by the events of 1968 to leave the Soviet Union and its history behind him. The Russian invasion of Czechoslovakia, as we have noted, freed him from the Soviet model and from Russian history—to which we may now add that May of 1968 in his own country also enabled him to begin anew. At the age of seventy, looking back at May '68, he willingly identified as an anarchist, with the proviso that "today's anarchy no longer has anything to do with the anarchy of 1890."[104]

After many years of looking abroad, either to Russia or the Third World, Sartre discovered that the student eruption in May 1968—an event that grew into a general strike, perhaps the most massive in scope of any in French history—had the effect of reorienting his energies. Now once again, as in the immediate postwar years, his attention was on France and the other advanced Western powers. He had returned to where he began.[105]

Student uprisings and wildcat strikes were so far removed from the agenda of the Communist party in France that its spokespersons responded unsympathetically and in tones that sounded downright conservative. No more than anyone else had Sartre foreseen the political explosions of May, but once they burst upon him he responded with an interview, subsequently converted into a pamphlet, titled "The Communists Fear Revolution." Sartre did not limit himself during the interview to accusing the Communists, in their willingness to settle for elections, of "objective complicity with de Gaulle."[106] He also expressed eagerness to learn new lessons from an uprising previously deemed "unthinkable,"[107] a rebellion occurring not under the circumstances of "need" that he had stressed in the first *Critique* but rather in a society of abundance, a "consumer society."[108] Obviously revolutionary strategy had to be rethought, although he warned that what might be learned in the West would probably have no meaning elsewhere. And even in the West, much of what happened in France, with its "strong anarchist tradition,"[109] might be of limited relevance in adjoining countries.

That Sartre was willing to consider in 1968 whatever the bearers of the black flag had to offer he proved beyond doubt when he sat down for an interview with student leader Daniel Cohn-Bendit, an admirer of Bakunin. Throughout the interview, it was Sartre who asked the questions and Cohn-Bendit who gave the answers; Sartre was the student, Cohn-Bendit the teacher.[110] Like Cohn-Bendit, like all the other anarchists of May, Sartre admired the "action committees" that brought together students with workers in 1968 and inevitably reminded him of the soviets of an earlier era. Nevertheless, a year later he rendered the judgment that May '68 failed because it "lacked political direction"; "it lacked a party capable of taking up completely the movement and its potentialities."[111]

Sartre in 1968 did indeed have it both ways and managed this feat, to his mind, without compromising himself. His previous historical examinations of revolution remained pertinent, his studies of Soviet history and the Third World were not to be withdrawn, but new events and new possibilities within the most economically advanced nations had now to be taken into account. A new chapter had to be added to the history of revolution; the historical project itself remained as vital as ever.

Chapter 6

History and a Note on Ethics

Anyone familiar with *Being and Nothingness* knows it closed with a tantalizing section bearing the title "Moral Perspectives." After raising a number of vital and enticing questions about ethics in the final three pages, Sartre ended his philosophical treatise with the sentence "We shall devote to [these matters] a future work." As everyone concedes, Sartre did not keep his promise of publishing a major work on ethics, but that has not prevented various scholars from trying to read one or another of his works, usually more imaginatively than convincingly, as if it were his ethics in all but name.[1]

Our claim is not to have unearthed a hidden, fully developed ethics in Sartre's most famous writings, nor do we intend to discuss his scattered comments on ethics in his final years.[2] Instead, what we wish to explore is what might have been, what at times almost was but admittedly never completely was; how he moved from an ahistorical and unworkable ethics shortly after World War II to a series of historically anchored reflections that he might have, but did not, systematize into a major contribution to moral and political philosophy in his *Critique of Dialectical Reason*.

History opened doors for Sartre; sometimes he walked through, sometimes not. In the case of history and ethics, he frequently traveled down a road that might have led somewhere well worth a visit, but never did he finish the journey. Repeatedly he spoke a language that sounded like a remarkable update of earlier theories of the social contract. At times, he came close to formulating an outline of a political and social revolution that would be marked by several historical stages, each accompanied intellectually by a complementary version of a social contract. The unwillingness of Sartre to grasp what was within his reach is our misfortune and perhaps his as well.

* * *

Sartre's original postwar groping toward an ethics was Kantian in inspiration and, like Kant's own ethics, ahistorical in orientation. He had pointed the way to his first explorations in moral philosophy in *Being and Nothingness,* where he had written that "for a long time the aim of ethics was to provide man with a way of *being."* All such ethical systems Sartre repudiated because they rested on the false claim that ethics could be founded on something given, fixed, ontologically sanctioned. Kant provided the welcome exception: "the Kantian morality is the first great ethical system which substitutes doing for being."[3]

It was in his well-known speech of 1945, "Existentialism Is a Humanism," that Sartre attempted to incorporate Kantian ethics into his philosophy. Kant had begun with the human subject and the human "will," not with an objective law of nature, and Sartre set out to do the same. As with Kant, moreover, Sartre would save from hopeless subjectivity and willfulness the moral choice of individual human beings by insisting that they universalize the maxim of their actions. "When a man commits himself to anything," said Sartre paraphrasing Kant, "he is not only choosing what he will be, but is thereby at the same time a legislator deciding for the whole of mankind."[4]

Unfortunately, no sooner had Sartre uttered his neo-Kantian words than they turned against him. In an application of his Kantian viewpoint, he said that if I marry and have children "I am thereby committing not only myself, but humanity as a whole, to the practice of monogamy." Quite obviously, he could not truly have meant what he said; his real point could only be that I have shown one human possibility, not that I have chosen monogamy for everyone else. Caught in a Kantian snare, Sartre struggled to escape but only made matters worse: "Everything happens," he continued, "to every man as though the whole human race had its eyes upon what he is doing and regulated its conduct accordingly." But is not the foregoing the ultimate Sartrean nightmare instead of an ethics? Is it not a world where the eyes of the Other and all the others are ever upon me, degrading me into an object?[5]

The most successful of Sartre's efforts in the mid-1940s to draw on Kantian rhetoric came in his essay *Anti-Semite and Jew.* There, as he gravitated toward politics, it is telling that while borrowing Kant's vocabulary, he in fact moved into a new non-Kantian ethical world. A Jew, he said, must act "as if all his acts were subject to a Kantian imperative": what would happen to Jews if all Jews acted as I do?[6] Sartre imposed a social and political context on Kant's individualistic and universalistic ethics, which is to say, he evolved to a position that was Kantian in name only. The categorical imperative was of little use to an *engagé* intellectual, out to reform the politics of France.

Even less was it of use to the political revolutionary Sartre would soon be. Merleau-Ponty in 1947 stated the position that Sartre would soon find impossible to avoid: "Once humanism attempts to fulfill itself with any consistency it becomes transformed into its opposite, namely, into violence," wrote Merleau-Ponty. Liberals wanting clean hands forget that "in advocating nonviolence one reinforces established violence." Before long, Sartre would accept Merleau-Ponty's affirmation that "Machiavelli is worth more than Kant."[7] If Sartre were to continue his search for an ethics, he would have to leave Kantian universalism behind, so as to come to terms with the specifics of politics, society, and history.[8]

One element of Kant's ethical thought that Sartre did retain over the years was the stress on "will." No longer, however, was the "will" that of the free human subject willing the categorical imperative. As Sartre's thought became more political, the "will" in question began to resemble that of the social contract.[9]

*   *   *

The most important Sartrean close encounter with theories of the social contract came in the *Critique of Dialectical Reason*; the very first encounter came thirty-three years earlier, 1927, in an essay titled "The Theory of the State in Modern French Thought." A mere twenty-two years old, Sartre proved he knew a thing or two about theories of the social contract when he wrote that "Natural right ... had since its original formulation by Grotius been developed into the finished form it had for the men of 1789. American and French revolutionaries gave natural right an actual existence and state sovereignty an ideal sanction."[10]

Exactly where Sartre stood on the social contract in his earliest years is not clear because his focus was elsewhere. The essay of 1927 addressed several thinkers of the Third Republic who wished as civil servants to impose a kind of syndicalism from above; they wanted to deemphasize the state and to reorient thought from politics to the economy. Corporatism and a functional division of labor were their themes rather than the authority of the French state. Not ethical reasoning but sociological analysis was the preoccupation of these more or less Durkheimian positivists; Sartre, however, would have nothing to do with the "realism" they wished to substitute for moral evaluation. As he put it, "He who sets out from *facts* will never end up with anything but facts."[11]

When Sartre, after a fourteen-year hiatus, returned to political thought during the War, it was not to set out from "facts" but rather to engage in the activity the Americans had hit upon during their revolution and that the French, following the American example, mimicked in 1789: the enactment of a social contract through the writing of a constitution. Meeting in secrecy with a group of intellectuals in 1941, Sartre took the position that he and his comrades needed to look beyond the present battle to the issue of how to give birth to a new postwar France. Accordingly, he drafted a one-hundred-page document, lost during the conflict but remembered by some of his cohort, a proposed new constitution that would have reshaped his country along the lines suggested by a reading of Proudhon and the anarcho-Syndicalists. Every trade and profession would be represented in the proposed legislature, and the financial worth of every object would be based on the amount of labor required to produce it.[12]

During the years immediately following the war, Sartre continued to advance notions inspired by Proudhon of a society based on an ongoing social contract. Nearly everything about Proudhon had, for some time, been of interest to Sartre, who in his war diaries had quoted with approval Proudhon's saying that "freedom ... can only exist and be apparent through constantly rejecting its own creations."[13] Much to Sartre's liking, Proudhon had denounced the constitutions of nineteenth-century France as the "tinsel of the circus" precisely because they were not founded on a genuine social contract. Not for Proudhon a social contract reminiscent of Pufendorf's, based on an illicit submission of subject to government rather than on a proper agreement between man and man. Also not for him, Locke's "tacit consent": Proudhon's would be an outspoken daily agreement among free men to secure and enhance their freedom, never an agreement by which they alienated their freedom, permitting someone to act for them. Nor would his contract be the narrowly political one of 1793. Economic rights were what truly mattered and these, far from being abstractions, must be the very soul of society. Everyday economic arrangements would be decided by a series of ongoing contractual arrangements; "the whole [would be] rebuilt upon the idea of contract," wrote Proudhon. The expression "sovereignty of the people" is hollow unless it means "an effective sovereignty of the working ... masses."[14]

Briefly in *Being and Nothingness* Sartre disagreed with what he took to be Proudhon's respect for private property, but that did not prevent him from appreciating Proudhon the contracturalist.[15] Proudhon was Sartre's man in 1941 when he wrote an anarcho-Syndicalist constitution, and he was again a favorite of Sartre six years later. The year 1947 was when Sartre remarked on how important it was for Marx's socialism to be offset by Proudhon's anarchism. In the same text, *What Is Literature?*, he entered a plea for what amounted to a social contract that would be renegotiated every day via the process of anarchist "permanent revolution" (see Chapter 5). Immediately thereafter he repeated in his notebooks the call for permanent revolution and the need to reinvent society continuously.[16] Anarchism and a radical reading of the social contract can readily go hand in hand and did so in Sartre's thought immediately after the war.

Sartre's notebooks of 1947 and 1948, although unsystematic and sprawling, did more with theories of the social contract than embrace their contemporary anarchistic advocates. Surveying the history of political thought, he sided with the contractual tradition and against its intellectual predecessors, divine right for one, patriarchalism for another, authoritarianism for a third, when he wrote "passive obedience does not exist since man cannot be passive. There is only obedience or revolt." Of special interest, he accused "the democratic state" of fostering a "contract of submission," an expression used by Pufendorf to justify absolutism by consent. Locke might appear on American banners, Rousseau on French, but Sartre seemed to be saying that modern liberal regimes come closer to Pufendorf's and Grotius's claims that rights and popular sovereignty were alienated long ago, permanently, for the sake of guaranteeing stability, than to Locke's inalienable natural rights and inalienable popular sovereignty.[17]

Whether a philosophy of the social contract can survive without a doctrine of rights is far from obvious, which raises the question of where rights fit in Sartre's intellectual schemes. What we can offer is the suggestion that after struggling with the idea of rights from the late 1930s to the late 1940s, Sartre eventually came around to siding with a reasonable facsimile. To say, as he did in his notebooks, that "the right of liberalism is ... mystification in its most pure form" is not necessarily a condemnation of all claims of rights. Nor is his statement that "the union of the oppressed will come about through violence and it will *always* contradict the existing right." Assertions of rights, he noted, were not the monopoly of the privileged: "all violence presents itself as the recuperation of a right and, reciprocally, every right inexorably contains within itself the embryo of violence." The larger point, enunciated in 1947, is that "man is by essence juridical, that is, he is not just a force but also a freedom."[18]

Sartre's position on rights, it seems, had evolved considerably since the late 1930s. At that time, Roquentin in *Nausea,* out to damn the bourgeoisie for refusing to face up to the contingency of existence, stated that "no one has rights" and, with perfect consistency, conceded that "I hadn't the right to exist."[19] Another hit, delivered again in the late 1930s, came with the publication of the short story "Childhood of a Leader," the tale of a protagonist who, faced like Roquentin with nothingness, joined a right-wing group and proclaimed "I exist because I have the right to exist."[20]

Obviously when Sartre became more sympathetic to rights a decade later, he could not ground them in nature or human nature or anything given *a priori.* Yet something resembling claims of rights did enter Sartre's thought in the postwar era from the moment he decided that existentialism was a humanism, human dignity a meaningful phrase, and freedom both something ontologically given and in need of political sanction (see Chapter 4). If this was not rights, it might as well have been. It speaks volumes that when Sartre sketched a journalistic account of revolutionary Cuba in 1960, he spoke frequently of the "rights" of the Cuban people.[21] And what he said of the Cubans he had been saying all along, now and again, about the victims of Western colonialism, whether in Latin America, Africa, or wherever. They, too, had rights, and he never tired of accusing the Western powers of violating those rights.[22]

*   *   *

It was in the *Critique of Dialectical Reason* that Sartre came closest to developing a novel application of theories of the social contract. Yet there were also moments in this text when he denied that notions of social contracts were what he had in mind.[23] Some students of Sartre's thought, drawing on his occasional nay-saying, have accordingly concluded that he wanted nothing to do with the social contract.[24]

Before dismissing the possibility that Sartre's thought had ties to social contract theory, we should recognize how potentially embarrassing it would have been to admit an affinity with such theorizing on the part of a thinker who had spent so many years trying to establish his credentials as a Marxist thinker, Marxism wanting nothing to do with theories of the social contract other than to denounce them as bourgeois mystification. When the worker rose up in the nineteenth century, remarked Sartre in good Marxian fashion, the bourgeoisie asked, "Had he not broken the social compact?"[25]Furthermore, wanting to identify as a savior of Marxist thought, Sartre could not admit in the *Critique* his affinities with Proudhon and the anarchists, purveyors of left-wing notions of a social contract. The rule of rules in the ranks of anarcho-Marxists, who typically claim to be "true" Marxists, is that one cannot concede a debt to anarchism.

Yet while Sartre might not have explicitly devoted his efforts to making a contribution to social contract theory, he repeatedly opened the possibility of such an intellectual undertaking. The sentence in which he denied that his was a social contract is followed by these words: "We are not trying to describe the basis of particular societies …; we are trying to explain the necessary transition from an immediate form of [revolutionary] group which is in danger of dissolution to another form, which is reflexive but permanent."[26] That is, Sartre's efforts were devoted to a general discussion of the changing conditions under which a revolutionary group might form and then sustain itself. Freedom asserted individually and collectively against oppression, freedom alienated to save the revolution, freedom regained at a later date were his concerns. One by one he discussed different phases of the revolutionary process, each of which, if he dared, could have been conceptually reformulated as a new version of the social contract for a new situation—a revolution occurring in several moments, with several corresponding contracts.

Certainly his pervasive usage of terminology that coincided with the traditional vocabulary of social contract theory is striking: "constituent" and "constituted" power, "consent," "constitution," "sovereignty," "authority," "legitimacy" are words that recur throughout his text. Commenting on Sartre's *Critique*, Raymond Aron may have offered valuable insights when he wrote that "free *praxis* constitutes the [Sartrean] equivalent of the *state of nature* of classical seventeenth-century philosophers," and again when he likened the phase Sartre called "institution" to "the *civil society* of the seventeenth-century philosophers."[27]

Throughout the first volume of the *Critique of Dialectical Reason*, Sartre cited many historical examples, usually drawn from the French Revolution, such as the seizing of the Bastille, the Tennis Court Oath, the struggle between Jacobins and Montagnards, or the Terror. He did not, however, pretend to be writing the history that would supposedly come to fruition only later, in volume two. His account of revolution was formal and abstract, consisting of a delineation of the several phases through which revolutionary groups might form or falter, and of their possible transformation from one type of structure to another, as they struggled to survive. First there was the "series," next the "oath," followed by the "organization," and then the "institution."

No matter what phase of group formation or decomposition Sartre was discussing, he always accorded the individual person a privileged status. The more he stressed the group, the more adamantly he denied it ontological status, to the chagrin of some very thoughtful students of his philosophy. Probably the most common explanation is that Sartre was "the last of the Cartesians."[28] One scholar after another has made the case that Sartre was unconvincing in his efforts to depict a collective social world by adding individual to individual.[29] While we share the point of view of Sartre's critics, our contention is that much, perhaps everything, would fall into place if we thought of Sartre's efforts as attempts, never admitted, never fulfilled, to conceive of the revolutionary process as a succession of social contracts, some signed under highly adverse conditions, by individuals acting on the basis of free if highly constrained choice.

Sartre's starting point was the transition of individuals from "seriality" to the "group-in-fusion," that is, from socially induced isolation to spontaneous bonding in the face of an external threat. His favorite example from the French Revolution was the seizure of the Bastille, which permitted him to indulge, as we have noted (see Chapter 5), his suppressed anarchist impulses. We may now add that the flight to the Bastille was also a perfect example of a social contract signed by individuals, none of whom thereby alienated freedom to someone else. Another example was the Cuban revolution in the early days when "this broken, atomized society" shook off the yoke, and the oppressed populace engaged in a "revolution continually in action," never permitting anyone to become "an incumbent in his post," and refused to succumb to the demands of a theory or ideology.[30] Each time Sartre cited historical evidence of a group-in-fusion, he experienced the joys of revisiting, in effect, his call for permanent revolution and a daily renegotiation of the social contract in *What Is Literature?* (see Chapter 5), but with the advantage of grounding his early fanciful vision in actual historical experience.

Sooner or later, usually sooner, the group-in-fusion finds that because it lacks formal organization, its members must either fall back into seriality or move on to a new phase, marked by threats coming from within rather than without. To preserve the group, the various individuals choose to take an "oath" or make a "pledge" (*serment*) to one another, promising fidelity to the movement and agreeing to be forced to be free if they stray. The Tennis Court Oath and Rousseau come to mind,[31] so does the Terror insofar as each person agrees to be terrorized if he or she reneges on a promise made. Fraternity and terror are one and the same in what might be considered a second type of social contract, far less innocent than the first. "Fraternity is expressed in the group by a set of reciprocal and individual obligations, defined by the whole group."[32] Terror, whether physical or psychological, is what is necessary to uphold the revised social contract.

At every stage of the evolution of the group from one form to the next, Sartre spoke in terms of the "constituting" dialectic of the individual and the "constituted" dialectic of the social whole, never of the social whole as a "hyper-organism." Always it was a matter of individuals and their agreements, although individuals find themselves in less and less control as they enter the phases of "organization" and "institution." More and more, in the terminology of social contract, the question will be whether united individuals have alienated their sovereignty, and if they have, whether it can ever be reclaimed.

Sartre had been struggling with the question of the alienation of sovereignty well in advance of the *Critique,* as when he wrote eight years earlier that "the splitting up of the proletariat corresponds to a breaking apart of popular sovereignty."[33] Again, when de Gaulle assumed power in 1958, Sartre denounced a violation of popular sovereignty: "It is not up to de Gaulle to create the Fifth Republic. It is up to the French people themselves in their full and entire sovereignty."[34] In the *Critique,* however, as Sartre moved beyond the group-in-fusion to address the subsequent phases of "pledge," organization, and institution, he found that the question of sovereignty was difficult to answer.

By itself, the "pledge" is not enough to prevent the group from collapsing. An organization is needed, which eventually must become an institution. Once individuals form an organization, collective forces begin to take over the movement, and the individuals are served but their freedom curtailed. Under the new dispensation, an individual must perform a particular function for the sake of the whole. Duties are a feature of this phase of the process; rights are defined by the role one plays in the structure. Perhaps most tellingly, the principle of generational autonomy is forfeited: "From birth onwards, the arrival of the child in the milieu of the pledge is the equivalent for him of making a pledge."[35] This is the kind of provision that one finds in Pufendorf's conservative social contract and against which Locke and his progeny rebelled in the name of generational autonomy.

The conservative turn of the structured group, and of what might serve as its revised social contract, comes to fruition when the collectivity evolves into an "institution." At this point, the forward movement of the individual members has ground to a halt, inertia has taken over; authority appears as a solution and manifests itself in a firm distinction between leaders and led.

The "common individual" has become an "institutional individual," who is immediately suspect if he or she questions authority. Throughout this part of his presentation, Sartre frequently speaks of "sovereignty" and of what looks very much like a transfer of sovereignty from people to rulers. Here again, Sartre's thought paralleled that of the conservative theorists of the social contract, Grotius and Pufendorf, who spoke of an alienation of sovereignty from people to ruler, absolutism by consent.

Sartre came perilously near to formulating his own doctrine of absolutism by consent in the second volume of the *Critique*. For Pufendorf, it was a monarch who would incarnate sovereignty; for Sartre, it was, disturbingly, Stalin. In a section on the "incarnation of the sovereign in an individual," Sartre wrote that Stalin *"is the only one through whom this serialization can be dissolved and the groups reconstituted."*[36]

It is tempting to suggest that Sartre replayed in reverse order the entire history of social contract tradition from Grotius and Pufendorf through Locke and beyond. Whereas Sartre's predecessors began with absolutism (Grotius and Pufendorf) but ended with freedom (Locke), Sartre, with an eye on the French and Russian revolutions, began with freedom and ended with absolutism.

Grotius and Pufendorf, frightened by wars of religion, posited natural rights and popular sovereignty as alienable and in fact alienated long ago to achieve stability. Locke famously countered at a later date with his notion of inalienable rights and inalienable sovereignty, and some of his offspring, Tom Paine for one but anarchists most of all, further radicalized his thought.

Sartre, quite distinctively, started with individuals and populace in charge, acting on the basis of what amounted to a radical social contract; subsequently, however, the original contract was transformed time and again in an ever more authoritarian direction, with the consenting people cast as passive followers and the ruler free to do as he pleased. "By means of sovereignty," he wrote in volume one of the *Critique*, "the group alienates itself to a single man."[37] In volume two, Stalin figured as this single man, the "incarnation" of the Russian people during the period when he was dictatorially building the modern economy at horrendous human cost.

* * *

Sartre apparently was uncomfortable with the direction of his thought and tried by several means to distance himself from the implications of his position. One strategy was to emphasize the ambiguity of consent and legitimacy. Hence we find him remarking of the one-man ruler that "his power is not based on consent (as a positive act of adhesion) but rather consent to his power is an interiorization of the impossibility of resisting it." Again: "Something like acceptance … confers serial pseudo-legitimacy on the sovereign." His acts may be arbitrary but "this is far from preventing orders from being seen as *legitimate.*"[38]

Alternatively, Sartre sought to neutralize the issues of consent and legitimacy raised in social contract theory by deeming them irrelevant to the brutal world we inhabit: "within a given society, the State cannot be said to be either legitimate or illegitimate." All we can say is that's how things are. Bolshevik rule, too, he assures us, was "neither legitimate nor illegitimate."[39] Yet he could not unburden himself consistently of the notion of legitimacy; in 1965, he remarked that "an analysis of the notion of legitimacy is what was lacking in *The Communists and Peace.*"[40]

Perhaps Sartre's best effort to distance himself in the first *Critique* from what Stalin did to Bolshevism came when he stated that the time had arrived for "debureaucratization, decentralization, and democratization." Because "the destruction of the Soviet bourgeoisie was completed long ago," the hour had struck for the sovereign to "abandon monopoly of the group."[41] Even at his most apologetic when dealing with Russia, Sartre held on to the claim that sovereignty ultimately belongs to the people and is always theirs to reclaim.[42]

Thus, eight years in advance, Sartre had prepared the way for his statement in response to May '68: "Why I mostly reproach people who insult the students is that they fail to see that the students are trying to express a new claim, the right of sovereignty. In a real democracy, all men must be sovereigns, that is, they must be allowed to decide what to do, not by themselves, each in his own corner, but in the company of others."[43] Several years after May '68, when Sartre deemed the French people once again "atomized," he continued to express the hope that they would "rediscover deep within themselves their need for freedom and sovereignty."[44]

Sartre never came to terms with social contract theory, despite his incessant usage of its terminology and concepts. He began his ethics with a focus on Kantian "will" rather than "being." He might have fulfilled his ethics with reflections on will as social contract, will as caught up in different contracts for different circumstances, always heading back to a resumption in new terms of the freedom of the first contract. Had he done so, he would not have had to postpone his ethics until after the revolution; he could have made ethics out of the revolution itself. The door was open but Sartre, ever preoccupied with his Marxist credentials, did not enter.

* * *

Never did Sartre explicitly embrace social contract theory but neither, it seems, could he ever be done with it. It is still very much on his mind, or at least at the back of his mind, in his study of Flaubert. Throughout the massive three volumes "consent" continued to figure in Sartre's vocabulary, as when he suggested that Flaubert was "a young man who regarded himself as an outcast, constituted without his consent by his mother's austerity." Flaubert himself, noted Sartre, mentioned "consent" when commenting on his self-inflicted illness: "I am really rather well since consenting to be always ill." Sartre also spoke of a "social contract" when discussing Flaubert's convalescence: "he demands that a familial pact and a social contract acknowledge that in his room he is 'at home.'" Much later in Flaubert's life, at the time of the fall of the Second Empire and advent of the Third Republic, Sartre found his subject applying the "social contract" to public life: according to Sartre, Flaubert thought the French people had wrongly broken the "contract" with their dictator. Speaking in his own voice, Sartre held it against the back door Third Republic that it "established itself illicitly, shamefully, and *without a constitution,*" and he castigated Flaubert for calling this a "fortunate absence of principles."[45]

As rhetoric, the social contract flourished in Sartre's writings across the decades and never exited his thought. As theory, it was perpetually an understudy in his philosophical and historical presentations, never an actor permitted to perform before an audience—this despite its great promise.

* * *

Sartre is fascinating not only for the questions he asked and answered. Also tantalizing and frustrating are the questions he never quite answered, such as the relationship between human history and the "human condition" (see Chapter 4), and the questions he flirted with but never explicitly posed, such as where the theory of the social contract might fit in his historical thought and whether it might have served as an essential element in the ethics he never wrote. Our consolation must be that even as unfinished business, his encounters with history never fail to challenge, provoke, and illuminate.

Even if Sartre left much work unfinished, there are reasons to hope he may be of assistance to us as we struggle to answer our own questions. In the course of investigating Sartre's encounters with Clio, we have attempted to make contributions to intellectual, cultural, and political history; that is to say, we have examined the past. But the Sartre of our study is possibly pertinent to our day as well. Biography is staging a scholarly resurgence in our time, and who better to consult about the writing of biography than Sartre? The links between writing fiction and writing history are also prominent among our current preoccupations, and again, who better than Sartre to argue with or against? If scholars have moved from modern to postmodern, from history as truth to history as story, then Sartre may well be worth another look—he who reversed our trajectory, beginning as a postmodernist *avant la lettre* in *Nausea,* but then evolved away from that perspective in his later works.

The vogue of Sartre of times past may well be over but so, too, is the revulsion against Sartre of more recent times, when French intellectuals, repenting of the postwar years of fellow traveling, made it their business to excoriate Sartre on every possible occasion. Today, there are signs that scholars and students are approaching Sartre anew, asking different questions from those posed by earlier generations and sometimes finding clues to answers in the writings of Jean-Paul Sartre.

Notes

Chapter 1

1. Annie Cohen-Solal, *Sartre: A Life* (Pantheon Books, 1987), p. xiii.
2. Sartre, *Critique of Dialectical Reason,* vol. 1 (London: Verso, 1982), p. 69. Here, as elsewhere throughout the ensuing chapters, for the French I have used *Critique de la Raison Dialectique* (Paris: Gallimard, 1960).
3. Sartre, "The Purpose of Writing" in *Between Existentialism and Marxism* (New York: Pantheon Books, 1983), p. 9.
4. Still serviceable after all these years on the topic of struggles within the French left is George Lichtheim, *Marxism in Modern France* (New York: Columbia University Press, 1966).
5. Ronald E. Santoni, *Bad Faith, Good Faith, and Authenticity in Sartre's Early Philosophy* (Philadelphia: Temple University Press, 1995).
6. E.g., his comments on ethics in the interviews held a month before his death, published under the title *Hope Now: the 1980 Interviews* (Chicago: University of Chicago Press, 1996). Simone de Beauvoir repudiated these last minute interviews, but some scholars find them compelling. E.g., Ronald E. Santoni, *Sartre and Violence: Curiously Ambivalent* (University Park: Pennsylvania State University Press, 2003), p. 166. See also Ronald Aronson's introduction to *Hope Now,* "Sartre's Last Words," pp. 3–40.
7. Quoted by Cohen-Solal, *Sartre,* p. 412.
8. Sartre, *La Nausée* (Paris: Gallimard, 1938) Folio edition (1987), pp. 104, 143.
9. Ibid., pp. 104, 103, 99, 106.
10. Ibid., pp. 64, 104.
11. Ibid., pp. 30, 87.
12. Ibid., pp. 90, 30, 65, 66.
13. Sartre, *Life/Situations* (New York: Pantheon Books, 1977), p. 44.
14. *Witness to My Life: the Letters of Jean-Paul Sartre to Simone de Beauvoir, 1926–1939* (New York: Charles Scribner's Sons, 1992), p. 316.
15. *The War Diaries of Jean-Paul Sartre: November 1939/March 1940* (New York: Pantheon Books, 1984), p. 185.

16. Simone de Beauvoir, *La Force de l'Âge* (Paris: Gallimard, 1960) Folio edition (1976–1977), pp. 410, 415, 424.

17. *La Nausée,* pp. 21, 153.

18. *La Force de l'Âge,* p. 182.

19. Ibid., p. 25.

20. Ibid., p. 246. *La Nausée,* p. 127. *Life/Situations,* p. 45.

21. *La Force de l'Âge,* p. 629.

22. Ibid., p. 410.

23. *Witness to My Life,* pp. 233, 270.

24. Sartre, *Situations* (New York: George Braziller, 1965), p. 178.

25. Quoted by Cohen-Solal, *Sartre,* pp. 150, 151.

26. *Life/Situations,* p. 45.

27. Sartre, "Itinerary of a Thought" in *Between Existentialism and Marxism,* p. 34.

28. *Life/Situations,* pp. 44–45.

29. Simone de Beauvoir, *Adieux: A Farewell to Sartre* (New York: Pantheon Books, 1984), p. 399.

30. Simone de Beauvoir, *La Force des Choses,* vol. 2 (Paris: Gallimard, 1963) Folio edition (1977–1978), p. 489.

31. *Witness to My Life,* p. 318.

32. Sartre, quoted by de Beauvoir, *Adieux,* p. 168.

Chapter 2

1. Sartre, *La Nausée* (Paris: Gallimard, 1938) Folio edition (1987), pp. 53, 139.

2. Heidegger, *Being and Time* (New York: Harper & Row, 1962), pp. 72, 253, 429, 449ff.

3. Raymond Aron, *History and the Dialectic of Violence: an Analysis of Sartre's Critique de la Raison Dialectique* (New York: Harper Torch Books, 1976), p. xii.

4. Ibid., pp. 6, 13–14.

5. Sartre, "La Nationalisation de la littérature" in *Situations, II* (Paris: Gallimard, 1948, 1975), pp. 40–41.

6. Ibid., pp. 41–42.

7. Dilthey spoke of "the problem of what I have called a Critique of Historical Reason." H. P. Rickman, ed., *Dilthey: Selected Writings* (Cambridge University Press, 1979), p. 207.

8. Sartre, "M. Mauriac et la liberté" *Situations, I* (Paris: Gallimard, 1947), pp. 44, 46–47, 48, 56–57.

9. Sartre, "*Sartoris* par W. Faulkner," "A propos de *Le Bruit et la Fureur*" in *Situations, I,* pp. 7–13, 70–81.

10. Sartre, "American Novelists in French Eyes," *Atlantic Monthly,* vol. 178 (July–December), 1946, pp. 114–118.

11. Sartre, "A propos de John Dos Passos et de *1919*" in *Situations, I,* pp. 14–25.

12. Sartre, *The Reprieve* (New York: Bantam, 1968), pp. 249, 251, 252.

13. Simone de Beauvoir, *La Force des Choses,* vol. 1 (Paris: Gallimard, 1963) Folio edition (1977–1978), pp. 360, 362.

14. de Beauvoir, "An American Renaissance in France," *The New York Times* (June 22, 1947), pp. 7, 29.

15. de Beauvoir, "Littérature et métaphysique" in *Les Temps Modernes,* vol. 1, no. 7 (1946), pp. 1153–1163.

16. Sartre, *The War Diaries of Jean-Paul Sartre: November 1939/March 1940* (New York: Pantheon Books, 1984), pp. 54–55, 146.

17. de Beauvoir, *La Force de l'Âge* (Paris: Gallimard, 1960) Folio edition (1976-77), pp. 497, 596.

18. Sartre, *War Diaries,* p. 182.

19. Sartre, *What Is Literature?* (New York: Harper Torch Books, 1965), pp. 232, 205n. For the French, here and throughout, I have used *Qu'est-ce que la littérature?* in *Situations, II* (Paris: Gallimard, 1948).

20. *La Nausée,* p. 213.

21. *What Is Literature?,* p. 233.

22. James Ceaser, "*Katastrophenhaft:* Martin Heidegger's America" in *Reconstructing America: the Symbol of America in Modern Thought* (New Haven: Yale University Press, 1997), ch. 8.

23. Sartre, "New York, the Colonial City" in *Literary and Philosophical Essays* (New York: Collier Books, 1962), p. 131.

24. de Beauvoir, *La Force des Choses,* vol. 1, p. 32.

25. Sartre, "Individualism and Conformism in the United States," "American Cities," "New York, the Colonial City" in *Literary and Philosophical Essays,* pp. 104–132.

26. "Individualism and Conformism," p. 109.

27. Sartre, "On the American Working Class," *Dissent* (Winter, 2001), pp. 25–37.

28. "American Cities," p. 125.

29. *What Is Literature?,* p. 232.

30. My focus is on Sartre's America as opposed to Heidegger's. For Camus's America versus Sartre's, the scholar to consult is Andy Martin, author of *The Boxer and the Goalkeeper: Sartre vs. Camus* (Hemel Hempstead: Simon & Schuster, 2012).

31. John B. Watson, *Behaviorism* (New Brunswick, NJ: Transaction Publishers, 1998), pp. 3–4.

32. Sartre, *Imagination: a Psychological Critique* (Ann Arbor: University of Michigan Press, 1962), p. 3.

33. Sartre, *The Transcendence of the Ego* (New York: Farrar, Straus and Giroux, n.d.).

34. *Being and Nothingness* (New York: Washington Square Press, 1966), p. 93. For the French, here and elsewhere, I have used *L'Être et le Néant* (Paris: Gallimard, 1943) Collection TEL 1987.

35. Watson, *Behaviorism,* pp. 6, 8, 11.

36. Sartre, *Being and Nothingness,* p. 716.

37. Ibid., p. 727.

38. Ibid., pp. 720, 726.

39. For a concise presentation of Freud's views on symbolism, see his *Introductory Lectures on Psycho-Analysis* (New York: W. W. Norton, 1989), ch. 10. Also, *The Interpretation of Dreams* (New York: Barnes and Noble, 1994), pp. 249–259.

40. *Being and Nothingness,* p. 732.

41. Ibid., pp. 578, 586, 713, 717. *La Nausée,* p. 17. Sartre was still using the example of "ambition" in the second *Critique. Critique of Dialectical Reason,* vol. 2 (London: Verso, 2006), p. 64. For the French, here as elsewhere throughout the volume, I have used *Critique de la Raison Dialectique: l'Intelligibilité de l'Histoire* (Paris: Gallimard, 1985).

42. *Being and Nothingness,* p. 93.

43. Ibid., p. 616.

44. For more on Sartre's take on Freud, a helpful source is Sartre, *The Freud Scenario* (Chicago: University of Chicago Press, 1985).

45. Sartre, "American Novelists in French Eyes," p. 114.

46. Sartre, "Explication de *L'Étranger*" in *Situations, I,* pp. 110, 109.

47. Albert Camus, *The Stranger* (New York: Vintage, 1946), p. 127.

48. Ibid., p. 52. *Being and Nothingness,* p. 797.

49. *The Stranger,* pp. 125, 137.

50. "Explication de *L'Étranger,*" pp. 120, 117.

51. Philip Thody's contention that Meursault "has gone through the experience of the absurd before the story begins" is directly contradicted by the evidence. *Albert Camus: A Study of His Work* (New York: Grove Press, 1957), p. 7.

52. "Explication", pp. 115, 116.

53. *What Is Literature?,* p. 126.

54. André Gide, *L'Immoraliste* (Mercure de France, 1902) Folio edition (1975), p. 60.

55. *Being and Nothingness,* p. 107.

56. Michel Contat and Michel Rybalka, *The Writings of Jean-Paul Sartre,* vol. 1 (Evanston: Northwestern University Press, 1974), p. 147.

57. *Dilthey: Selected Writings,* p. 93.

58. Ibid., p. 247.

59. Ibid., p. 260.

60. Ibid., pp. 94–95.

61. Ibid., p. 247. *Being and Nothingness,* pp. 727, 734.

62. *Dilthey,* pp. 259-260. *Being and Nothingness,* pp. 728, 733.

63. *Dilthey,* p. 259.

64. E.g., *Notebooks for an Ethics* (Chicago: University of Chicago Press, 1992), p. 489. *What Is Literature?,* pp. 209, 217, 233. *Between Existentialism and Marxism* (New York: Pantheon Books, 1975), p. 161. Cf. de Beauvoir, "Littérature et métaphysique," p. 1160.

65. Sartre, "On *The Idiot of the Family*" in *Life/Situations* (New York: Pantheon Books, 1977), p. 123.

66. *Being and Nothingness,* p. 768.

67. Ibid., pp. 734, 722.

68. Sartre, *Baudelaire* (New York: New Directions, 1950), pp. 16–19.

69. Ibid., pp. 79, 170, 42–43, 49.

70. Ibid., pp. 53, 57, 59, 66.

71. Ibid., pp. 15, 45–49, 51, 134.

72. Ibid., pp. 165, 167.

73. Ibid., p. 81.

74. Ibid., p. 84.

75. Sartre, *Saint Genet, Actor and Martyr* (New York: Pantheon Books, 1963), p. 49. On Genet and Sartre, a useful source is Richard N. Coe, *The Vision of Jean Genet* (New York: Grove Press, 1968).

76. Sartre, "The Itinerary of a Thought" in *Between Existentialism and Marxism* (New York: Pantheon Books, 1975), p. 35.

77. *La Force de l'Âge,* p. 665.

78. *Saint Genet,* p. 180.

79. Durkheim, *The Elementary Forms of the Religious Life* (New York: Free Press, 1965), p. 466.

80. Durkheim, *The Rules of Social Method* (New York: Free Press, 1965), ch. 3; *The Division of Labor in Society* (New York: Free Press, 1984), p. 40.

81. *Saint Genet,* pp. 601–606.

82. Ibid., p. 186.

83. Later, in 1959, he said that Genet was aware of his commitment. "The Purposes of Writing" in *Between Existentialism and Marxism,* p. 13.

84. Mark Poster offers a sympathetic account in *Existential Marxism in Postwar France: Sartre to Althusser* (Princeton University Press, 1975), pp. 195–201. Philip Thody delivers a withering critique in *Jean-Paul Sartre: A Literary and Political Study* (London: Hamish Hamilton, 1960), ch. 8.

85. *Being and Nothingness,* pp. 734, 768.

86. Nietzsche, *Beyond Good and Evil* (New York: Random House, 1966), no. 22.

87. Sartre, "The Itinerary of a Thought," pp. 42–43.

88. Ibid., p. 33. Sartre did not resist when his interlocutor pointed out that the study of Flaubert is marked by a vocabulary drawn from both earlier and later works.

89. Sartre, "Self-Portrait at Seventy" in *Life/Situations,* p. 47.

90. *Anti-Semite and Jew* (New York: Schocken Books, 1995), pp. 8, 55. "Présentation des *Temps Modernes*" in *Situations, II,* p. 19.

91. *Anti-Semite and Jew,* p. 37.

92. Ibid., p. 42.

93. Ibid., p. 35.

94. Mark Hulliung, *The Autocritique of Enlightenment* (Cambridge, MA: Harvard University Press, 1994), ch. 5.

95. Ibid., ch. 2.

96. "Présentation des *Temps Modernes*" p. 18.

97. Mark Hulliung, *Citizens and Citoyens: Republicans and Liberals in America and France* (Cambridge, MA: Harvard University Press, 2002), ch. 5.

98. Sartre, *Search for a Method* (New York: Knopf, 1963), p. 45.

99. Ibid., p. 152.

100. Ibid., pp. 127, 130, 144, 151, 156, 157, 176.

101. Ibid., p. 55.

102. Ibid., pp. 152–153, 29n–30n.

103. Ibid., pp. 29, 164.

104. *Critique of Dialectical Reason,* vol. 1 (London: Verso, 1982), p. 239. *Life/Situations,* p. 116.

105. *Critique of Dialectical Reason,* vol. 1, pp. 480–484. Lévi-Strauss responded by writing a repudiation of Sartre's views in *The Savage Mind* (Chicago: University of Chicago Press, 1966), ch. 9. On the participation of Lévi-Strauss in *Les Temps Modernes,* the work to consult is Howard Davies, *Sartre and "Les Temps Modernes"* (Cambridge University Press, 1987).

106. Sartre, "The Itinerary of a Thought," pp. 34, 35.

107. *La Nausée,* pp. 184–185. "Présentation des *Temps Modernes,*" p. 16. *Critique of Dialectical Reason,* vol. 1, pp. 446–449, 490, 581.

108. "Self-Portrait at Seventy," p. 45. *The Words* (New York: Vintage, 1981), p. 251.

109. *La Nausée,* pp. 71, 223.

110. *Being and Nothingness,* pp. 101–103. For the treatment of social roles in *Search for a Method,* pp. 105, 107, 130.

111. "Self-Portrait at Seventy," p. 45.

112. "La République du silence," *Situations, III* (Paris: Gallimard, 1949), pp. 11–14.

113. *Critique of Dialectical Reason,* vol. 1, pp. 95, 99–100, 256–269, 277–293, 677. *Search for a Method,* p. 80.

114. *Critique of Dialectical Reason,* vol. 1, pp. 39, 40, 52, 56, 65, 136, 216, 364, 407, 482, 583, 609, 635, 671, 678, 788, 803, 817–818.

115. *La Nausée,* pp. 30, 90. "On *The Idiot of the Family,*" pp. 112–113. "Sartre parle de Flaubert," *Magazine littéraire* (November 1976), pp. 97–98.

116. "On *The Idiot of the Family,*" p. 115.

117. *The Family Idiot,* vol. 3 (Chicago: University of Chicago Press, 1989), pp. 554, 609. A very able study is Hazel E. Barnes, *Sartre & Flaubert* (Chicago: University of Chicago Press, 1981).

118. *The Family Idiot,* vol. 5 (Chicago: University of Chicago Press, 1993), pp. 413, 454.

119. *The Emotions: Outline of a Theory* (Secaucus, NJ: Citadel Press, 1948). *Being and Nothingness,* p. 104.

120. *The Family Idiot,* vol. 1 (Chicago: University of Chicago Press, 1981), p. 438.

121. Ibid., vol. 5, p. 432.

122. *Critique of Dialectical Reason,* vol. 1, p. 69. *Critique of Dialectical Reason,* vol. 2, p. 16.

123. *The Family Idiot,* vol. 5, p. 387.

124. *Being and Nothingness,* p. 643.

125. *Search for a Method,* p. 90.

126. *Situations, IV* (Paris: Gallimard, 1964), p. 201. *Critique of Dialectical Reason,* vol. 2, p. 299.

127. A study that helps place Sartre in the context of Marxist thought, from Marx to Merleau-Ponty, is James Miller's *History and Human Existence* (Berkeley: University of California Press, 1979).

Chapter 3

1. Sartre, *Notebooks for an Ethics* (Chicago: University of Chicago Press, 1992), p. 32. These notes date from spring of 1947 to the fall of 1948.

2. Hegel, *The Philosophy of History* (New York: Dover, 1956), pp. 85–86.

3. Sartre, "Paris sous l'Occupation," *Situations, III* (Paris: Gallimard, 1949), pp. 28, 24.

4. Sartre, *Being and Nothingness* (New York: Washington Square Press, 1966), p. 797.

5. "La République du silence," *Situations, III,* pp. 11–14.

6. *Being and Nothingness,* pp. 523, 649, 672.

7. Nietzsche, *The Genealogy of Morals,* first essay, section 10.

8. Sartre, "Self-Portrait at Seventy," in *Life/Situations: Essays Written and Spoken* (New York: Pantheon, 1977), p. 5.

9. E.g., Simone de Beauvoir, *La Force de l'Âge* (Paris: Gallimard, 1960) Folio edition (1976–1977), p. 25; *La Force des Choses,* vol. 1 (Paris: Gallimard, 1963) Folio (1977), p. 16.

10. Marcus Aurelius, *Meditations* (New York: Penguin, 1975), p. 131.

11. Descartes, *Discourse on Method* in *Philosophical Works of Descartes* (New York: Dover, 1955), vol. 1, pp. 96–97. See also the fourth of his *Meditations.*

12. Sartre, "La Liberté Cartésienne," *Situations, I* (Paris: Gallimard, 1947), p. 319. *Being and Nothingness,* p. 484.

13. *Being and Nothingness,* p. 680.

14. Sartre, *Anti-Semite and Jew* (New York: Schocken, 1995), p. 93.

15. Ibid., pp. 18–19, 27, 54

16. Ibid., pp. 53, 17.

17. Sartre, *The Emotions: Outline of a Theory* (New York: Citadel Press, 1948), p. 37. Originally published, in French, in 1939.

18. *Anti-Semite and Jew,* pp. 17, 19.

19. Ibid., p. 27.

20. Ibid., p. 40.

21. Ibid., pp. 22–23, 32.

22. Ibid., p. 21.

23. Ibid., pp. 22–23.

24. Ibid., pp. 28, 13.

25. There was a moment early in his career when Sartre said "I may well end up a fascist if the reasoning that leads me there is correct." Clearly, however, he did not mean to be taken literally. Annie Cohen-Solal, *Sartre: a Life* (New York: Pantheon, 1987), p. 143.

26. *Anti-Semite and Jew,* pp. 66–67, 84, 91.

27. Ibid., pp. 69, 101.

28. Ibid., p. 67.

29. Ibid., pp. 98, 111, 119, 124, 129, 133.

30. Ibid., pp. 96–98, 127.

31. Ibid., pp. 90–91, 136–137.

32. *The War Diaries of Jean-Paul Sartre* (New York: Pantheon Books, 1984), p. 197.

33. *Being and Nothingness,* pp. 186, 567, 673.

34. Ibid., pp. 531, 711. Heidegger, *Being and Time* (New York: Harper Collins, 1962), pp. 174ff, 264, 271, 295, 300, 437, 466.

35. *Anti-Semite and Jew*, pp. 89–90.

36. Although the text of *Anti-Semite and Jew* features a strong display of the notion of "situation," it is worth noting that this concept may be found in Sartre's works at least as early as the *War Diaries*, pp. 329–330.

37. *La Force des Choses*, vol. 1, p. 69.

38. Sartre, *The Communists and Peace* (New York: George Braziller, 1968), pp. 185, 194, 210. This edition includes Sartre's "Reply to Claude Lefort," published initially in 1953. For the French text, I have used *Situations, VI* (Paris: Gallimard, 1964) and *Situations, VII* (Paris: Gallimard, 1965).

39. "Paris sous L'Occupation," p. 29.

40. *The Communists and Peace*, pp. 86–87.

41. Ibid., pp. 81, 242, 51.

42. Ibid., pp. 37, 28, 64, 24.

43. Ibid., pp. 37, 38, 51.

44. Ibid., p. 67.

45. Ibid., pp. 52, 54, 98.

46. Ibid., p. 52. *Anti-Semite and Jew*, p. 67 (as previously cited).

47. *The Communists and Peace*, pp. 174, 178, 127.

48. Ibid., pp. 133–137.

49. Ibid., pp. 149, 74.

50. Ibid., pp. 38, 210–211.

51. Ibid., pp. 193, 197.

52. Hannah Arendt, *The Origins of Totalitarianism* (New York: Harcourt, Brace, 1951).

53. *The Communists and Peace*, pp. 220, 124–125.

54. Ibid., pp. 52–53, 194.

55. Ibid., p. 85.

56. Ibid., p. 164.

57. Ibid., p. 145.

58. Ibid., pp. 167, 179.

59. Ibid., pp. 143, 184.

60. Ibid., pp. 179, 142.

61. Michel Crozier, *Le Phénomène Bureaucratique* (Paris: Editions du Seuil, 1963) and *La Société Bloquée* (Paris: Editions du Seuil, 1970). Stanley Hoffmann, "Paradoxes of the French Political Community," *In Search of France* (Cambridge, MA: Harvard University Press, 1963), pp. 1–117. On Crozier's less-than-happy connections with *Les Temps Modernes*, see Cohen-Solal, *Sartre*, p. 314. For an example of what he wrote for the magazine, see his essay on human engineering, published in July of 1951. For a critique of the claim that France was a stalemate society from 1900 to 1930, see Jean Touchard, *La Gauche en France depuis 1900* (Editions du Seuil, 1977), pp. 93–95.

62. E.g., *Critique of Dialectical Reason*, vol. 1 (London: Verso, 1982), pp. 759, 764. *The Family Idiot* (Chicago: University of Chicago Press, 1993), vol. 5, pp. 210, 220, 327.

63. E.g., *Critique of Dialectical Reason,* vol. 1, pp. 241–247, 510 (on "family capitalism"), 781–787.

64. The term "Third World" was apparently invented by Alfred Sauvy in 1952. In coining the term, he had in mind a parallel with "Third Estate."

65. *The Communists and Peace,* p. 201.

66. Sartre, "Colonialisme et néo-colonialisme" in *Situations, V* (Paris: Gallimard, 1964), pp. 32, 39.

67. Sartre, "Vietnam: Imperialism and Genocide" in *Between Existentialism and Marxism* (New York: Pantheon Books, 1975), pp. 70–71, 76–77.

68. Sartre, *Critique of Dialectical Reason,* vol. 1, p. 722.

69. Sartre, [introduction to Fanon] "Les Damnés de la terre" in *Situations, V,* pp. 176, 172.

70. *The Communists and Peace,* pp. 155.

71. Ibid., pp. 37, 54, 200–201, 214, 225.

72. Sartre, "Portrait du colonisé" in *Situations, V,* pp. 52–55.

73. Sartre, "Le Colonialisme est un système" in *Situations, V,* p. 44.

74. *The Communists and Peace,* p. 124. "Les Damnés," pp. 177, 178.

75. Frantz Fanon, *The Wretched of the Earth* (New York: Grove Press, 1982), p. 315.

76. Sartre, *Les Mouches* (Paris: Gallimard, 1947), Act 3, Scene 2.

77. "Les Damnés," pp. 178–179, 185.

78. Sartre, "Orphée noir" in *Situations, III,* p. 229.

79. Alexandre Kojève, *Introduction à la Lecture de Hegel* (Paris: Gallimard, 1947). TEL (1979).

80. Patrick Riley provides a good account of Kojève's (mis)reading of Hegel in "Introduction to the Reading of Alexandre Kojève," *Political Theory* (Feb., 1981), vol. 9, no. 1, 5–48. I agree with Michael Roth's point, that accuracy is not at issue. *Knowing and History: Appropriations of Hegel in Twentieth-Century France* (Ithaca: Cornell University Press, 1988), part two.

81. Hegel, *The Phenomenology of Mind* (New York: Harper & Row, 1967), p. 239.

82. *Being and Nothingness,* p. 474.

83. *La Force des Choses* (Paris: Gallimard, 1963) Folio (1978), vol. 2, p. 409.

84. Robert Coles, *Children of Crisis* (Boston: Little, Brown, 1967).

85. Fanon, *The Wretched of the Earth,* pp. 251, 37, 40, 94, 93.

86. "Les Damnés," pp. 178, 183–185.

87. There is a section on "The Black Man and Hegel" in *Black Skins, White Masks* (New York: Grove Press, 2008), pp. 191–197. But Fanon has relatively little to say about the dialectic of Master and Slave.

88. *Sartre on Cuba* (New York: Ballantine Books, 1961), pp. 38, 39, 43, 114, 116, 154, 157.

89. "Orphée noir," p. 237.

90. Ibid., pp. 237, 272, 276, 277.

91. "Paris sous l'Occupation," p. 41.

92. Sartre, *Qu'est-ce que la littérature?* in *Situations, II* (Paris: Gallimard, 1975), p. 124.

93. *Notebooks for an Ethics,* pp. 263, 331, 392, 405.

94. *Critique of Dialectical Reason,* vol. 1, pp. 331, 578n.

95. "Conversations with Jean-Paul Sartre, August-September, 1974" in Simone de Beauvoir, *Adieux: A Farewell to Sartre* (New York: Pantheon, 1984), pp. 351–352, 358, 361.

96. Ibid., p. 361.

97. *Huis Clos* (Paris: Gallimard, 1947) Folio (1987), scene 5, p. 85. *Being and Nothingness,* pp. 606–609.

98. *Being and Nothingness,* p. 782.

99. *La Nausée* (Paris: Gallimard, 1938) Folio (1987), p. 148.

100. *Notebooks for an Ethics,* p. 47.

101. *Adieux,* p. 326.

102. Quoted by Annie Cohen-Solal, *Sartre,* p. 203.

103. Simone de Beauvoir, *Le Deuxième Sexe* (Paris: Gallimard, 1976), vol. 1, p. 20.

104. Ibid., vol. 2 (Paris: Gallimard, 1976), pp. 644, 630.

105. Ibid., pp. 477, 480, 482, 484, 486.

106. Ibid., pp. 486, 511.

107. Ibid., p. 21.

108. Ibid., pp. 649, 484–485, 487.

Chapter 4

1. Sartre, *Between Existentialism and Marxism* (New York: Pantheon Books, 1975), p. 29. Sartre, *Notebooks for an Ethics* (Chicago: University of Chicago Press, 1992), pp. 23, 40, 122.

2. Sartre, *L'Existentialisme est un Humanisme* (Paris: Nagel, 1970), p. 67.

3. Sartre, *What Is Literature?* (New York: Harper & Row, 1965), pp. 150–151.

4. Ibid., p. 209.

5. Sartre, *Being and Nothingness* (New York: Washington Square Press, 1966), p. 688.

6. Sartre, *La Nausée* (Paris: Gallimard, 1938) Folio (1987), p. 64.

7. To my mind, Martin Esslin's study, *The Theatre of the Absurd* (Baltimore: Penguin Books, 1976), ch. 1, has stood the test of time for its thoughtful commentary on Beckett.

8. *La Nausée,* p. 183.

9. Esslin, *The Theatre of the Absurd,* p. 60.

10. Samuel Beckett, *Waiting for Godot* (New York: Grove Press, 1954), p. 52a.

11. Ibid., p. 50a. "Time flows again already."

12. Ibid., pp. 33a, 33b, 34a, 58b.

13. *Being and Nothingness,* pp. 100, 348, 400, 785.

14. *La Nausée,* pp. 184–185. *Godot,* pp. 39a, 41b.

15. *Godot,* pp. 11b, 35a, 40a.

16. Ibid., pp. 9a, 31b, 44b, 53b, 57b.

17. *Godot,* pp. 7a, 8a, 8b, 14b, 16a, 27b, 34b.

18. *La Nausée,* pp. 213, 243.

19. Michel Contat and Michel Rybalka, eds., *The Writings of Jean-Paul Sartre,* vol. 1 (Evanston: Northwestern University Press, 1974), p. 404.

20. Simone de Beauvoir, *La Force des Choses* (Paris: Gallimard, 1963) Folio (1978), vol. 2, p. 34.

21. Ibid., vol. 2, p. 460.

22. Simone de Beauvoir, *Le Deuxième Sexe* (Paris: Gallimard, 1976), vol. 2, p. 494.

23. Sartre, "D'une Chine à l'autre" in *Situations, V* (Paris: Gallimard, 1964), pp. 12, 20, 21.

24. Sartre, *The Family Idiot* (Chicago: University of Chicago Press, 1981), vol. 1, pp. 527, 555.

25. Sartre, "La République du silence," *Situations, III* (Paris: Gallimard, 1949), p. 11–12.

26. Sartre, *Anti-Semite and Jew* (New York: Schocken Books, 1995), pp. 60, 54.

27. Ibid., p. 60.

28. Ibid., pp. 91, 136, 138. *Réflexions sur la Question Juive* (Paris: Paul Morihien, 1946), pp. 117, 178, 180.

29. *Being and Nothingness*, p. 784.

30. *La Nausée*, p. 225.

31. Esslin, *The Theatre of the Absurd*, p. 46.

32. Sartre, *Huis Clos* (Paris: Gallimard, 1947) Folio edition (1987), scene 1, p. 15.

33. *La Nausée*, p. 162.

34. Ibid., p. 172.

35. Ibid., p. 170.

36. Sartre, *L'Existentialisme est un Humanisme*, pp. 22, 37.

37. Sartre, *The Words* (New York: Vintage, 1981), p. 212.

38. Sartre, *Between Existentialism and Marxism*, p. 34.

39. "La République du silence," p. 13.

40. *Anti-Semite and Jew*, p. 90.

41. *Notebooks for an Ethics*, pp. 73–76.

42. *What Is Literature?*, pp. 209, 214, 215.

43. Ibid., pp. 214–216.

44. Ibid., p. 217n.

45. *Vol de Nuit* in *Oeuvres de Saint-Exupéry* (Paris: Gallimard, 1953), p. 108. Cf. p. 98, where he speaks of "*cette lutte*" and of "*des cités qui tombaient.*"

46. As Sartre remembered his childhood, even then he was fascinated by Flaubert, the Goncourts, and Gautier. *The Words*, p. 179.

47. Simone de Beauvoir, *The Ethics of Ambiguity* (Secaucus: Citadel Press, 1948), pp. 7–10.

48. *What Is Literature?*, p. 28.

49. Ibid., pp. 20, 28, 69, 81, 110, 169.

50. Montaigne, *Essais,* vol. 3 (Paris: Garnier-Flammarion, 1979), p. 20. Bk. 3, essay 2.

51. *Essais,* vol. 2, pp. 9, 10–11. Bk. 2, essay 1.

52. *Essais,* vol. 3, p. 20. Bk. 3, essay 2.

53. *What Is Literature?*, pp. 28, 181.

54. Sartre, *Critique of Dialectical Reason,* vol. 1 (London: Verso, 1982), pp. 52, 64, 69.

55. *What Is Literature?*, pp. 8, 13, 17, 151, 174, 185, 190, 215, 216, 221, 244n, 265, 272.

56. Ibid., p. 28.

57. Pascal, *Pensées* (Paris: Garnier-Flammarion, 1976), nos. 347, 348, 349, 426.

58. *Notebooks for an Ethics,* p. 21.

59. Ibid., p. 494. *Pensées,* no. 206.

60. *What Is Literature?,* pp. 20, 28, 69, 81, 110.

61. Ibid., p. 169. *Pensées,* no. 93.

62. *Essais,* vol. 3, pp. 260–261. Bk. 3, essay 12.

63. *Pensées,* no. 469.

64. Ibid., no. 72.

65. Ibid., nos. 72, 252, 67.

66. Ibid., no. 127.

67. *Waiting for Godot,* pp. 44b ("diversion" in *En Attendant Godot*; "occupation" in Beckett's English translation), 52a, 56a.

68. *Pensées,* nos. 164, 131

69. Ibid., no. 172.

70. *Essais,* vol. 2, p. 289. Bk. 2, essay 16.

71. *Pensées,* nos. 377, 144.

72. "Orphée noir" in *Situations, III* (Paris: Gallimard, 1949), p. 274.

73. *Sartre on Cuba* (New York: Ballantine Books, 1961), pp. 100, 148.

74. *The Family Idiot,* vol. 1 (University of Chicago Press, 1981), pp. 141, 200–202, 249, 345, 500, 618; vol. 3 (Chicago: University of Chicago Press, 1989), p. 407; vol. 4 (Chicago: University of Chicago Press, 1991), pp. 297, 298; vol. 5 (Chicago: University of Chicago Press, 1993), pp. 83, 315.

75. Ibid., vol. 3, pp. 397, 399, 400, 403.

76. André Malraux, *Anti-Memoirs* (Holt, Rinehart, Winston, 1968), p. 7. *Les Noyers de l'Altenburg* (Paris: Gallimard, 1948), pp. 98–99.

77. *Anti-Memoirs,* p. 8.

78. André Malraux, *La Condition Humaine* (Paris: Gallimard, 1946) Folio (1975), pp. 9–10, 17, 50, 59, 130.

79. Ibid., pp. 79, 90, 256.

80. *What Is Literature?,* p. 205n.

81. Annie Cohen-Solal, *Sartre: A Life* (New York: Pantheon, 1987), pp. 274, 331. *Writings of Jean-Paul Sartre,* vol. 1, p. 267. Camus's reviews of *La Nausée* and *Le Mur* have been reprinted in *Essais de Albert Camus* (Paris: Gallimard, Pléiade, 1965), pp. 1417–1422.

82. Camus, *La Peste* (Paris: Gallimard, 1947) Folio (1972), pp. 251, 183.

83. *Pensées,* no. 199. *La Peste,* p. 298.

84. *La Nausée,* pp. 183–184. *Le Mythe de Sisyphe* (Paris: Gallimard, 1942) NRF edition (1971), *passim.*

85. *La Nausée,* pp. 183, 186, 239, 246. Albert Camus, *The Stranger* (New York: Vintage, 1946), p. 105.

86. *The Stranger,* p. 52. *Le Mythe de Sisyphe,* p. 86.

87. *Sisyphe,* p. 17.

88. Simone de Beauvoir, *La Force de l'Âge* (Paris: Gallimard, 1960) Folio (1976–1977), pp. 37, 40, 89, 128–129, 154–156.

89. *Sisyphe,* p. 76.

90. *La Peste,* pp. 208, 162.

91. *La Peste,* p. 94.

92. Ibid., pp. 253, 218.

93. Sartre was a founder of the short-lived *Rassemblement Démocratique Révolution-naire* that sided with neither America nor Russia. The relevant text is Sartre, David Rousset, Gérard Rosenthal, *Entertiens sur la politique* (Paris: Gallimard, 1949).

94. Albert Camus, *The Rebel* (New York: Vintage, 1984), pp. 289, 16. For the French, I have used *L'Homme Révolté* (Paris: Gallimard, 1951).

95. Ibid., p. 22.

96. *Sisyphus,* p. 88. *The Stranger,* p. 127. *La Peste,* p. 183. *The Rebel,* p. 304.

97. *The Rebel,* pp. 94n (the English translation omits "the Fathers"), 186–187, 193, 196, 205, 210, 222, 233, 234.

98. Francis Jeanson, "Albert Camus or The Soul in Revolt" in David A. Sprintzen and Adrian van den Hoven, *Sartre and Camus: A Historic Confrontation* (Amherst, NY: Humanity Books, 2004), pp. 82, 83, 87, 94, 95. This book contains all the relevant documents plus commentary.

99. Jeanson, "To Tell You Everything" in *Sartre and Camus,* pp. 171, 174, 176, 178, 181, 188.

100. Ibid., p. 190.

101. Sartre, "Reply to Albert Camus" in *Sartre and Camus,* pp. 132, 144, 146, 152, 153.

102. Sartre, *Situations, I* (Paris: Gallimard, 1947), p. 101. "Reply to Albert Camus," p. 149. *Situations* (New York: George Braziller, 1965), pp. 109–110.

103. Sartre, "Présentation des *Temps Modernes*" in *Situations, II* (Paris: Gallimard, 1948; reissued on 1975), pp. 22, 15.

104. *L'Existentialisme est un Humanisme,* p. 79.

105. *What Is Literature?,* p. 209. *Notebooks for an Ethics,* p. 489.

106. Sartre, *Saint Genet: Actor and Martyr* (New York: Pantheon, 1963), pp. 50, 320, 255. See also pp. 370, 597.

107. Sartre, *Critique of Dialectical Reason,* vol. 2 (New York: Verso, 1991), p. 203.

108. See, for example, *The Family Idiot* (Chicago: University of Chicago Press, 1981–1993), vol. 1, pp. 433, 434, 569–570, 573; vol. 2, p. 184; vol. 3, pp. 448, 528; vol. 5, pp. 153, 284.

109. Ibid., vol. 3, p. 322; vol. 5, p. 381.

110. Sartre, "Kierkegaard: the Singular Universal" in *Between Existentialism and Marxism,* p. 161.

Chapter 5

1. Fredric Jameson, "Foreword" to Sartre, *Critique of Dialectical Reason,* vol. 2 (New York: Verso: 2006), p. xxi.

2. *Critique of Dialectical Reason,* vol. 2, p. 164n. For the original French, see *Critique de la Raison dialectique,* vol. 2 (Paris: Gallimard, 1985), p. 177n.

3. Sartre, "Le Réformisme et les fétiches," *Les Temps Modernes,* vol. 11, pt. 2 (January–June, 1956), p. 1158.

4. *Critique of Dialectical Reason,* vol. 2, pp. 121, 187.

5. Sartre, quoted by Simone de Beauvoir, *Adieux* (New York: Pantheon, 1984), p. 370.

6. Raymond Aron, *L'Opium des Intellectuels* (Paris: Calmann-Lévy, 1955).

7. Maurice Merleau-Ponty, *Humanism and Terror* (Boston: Beacon Press, 1969), p. 153.

8. Sartre, *The Ghost of Stalin* (New York: George Braziller), p. 121.

9. "Le Réformisme et les fétiches," p. 1158.

10. Albert Camus, *The Rebel* (New York: Vintage, 1991), pp. 20, 28.

11. Simone de Beauvoir, *La Force de l'Âge* (Paris: Gallimard, 1960) Folio (1976–1977), p. 156.

12. Raymond Aron, *La Sociologie Allemande Contemporaine* (Paris: Alcan, 1935) and *Introduction à la Philosophie de l'Histoire: Essai sur les Limites de l'Objectivité Historique* (Paris: Gallimard, 1938).

13. Simone de Beauvoir, *La Force des Choses,* vol. 1 (Paris: Gallimard, 1963) Folio (1977), p. 135.

14. Raymond Aron, *History and the Dialectic of Violence* (New York: Harper TorchBooks, 1976), p. xviii.

15. Sartre, "Merleau-Ponty" in *Situations, IV* (Paris: Gallimard, 1964), p. 194.

16. Maurice Merleau-Ponty, *Les Aventures de la Dialectique* (Paris: Gallimard, 1955), pp. 329–330.

17. Simone de Beauvoir, "La Pensée de droite, aujourd'hui," *Les Temps Modernes,* vol. 10, pt. 2 (March–July, 1955), p. 1539.

18. There is some evidence that Sartre from early on was inclined to think of Aron as a second-rate thinker. On December 27, 1939, he wrote to Simone de Beauvoir, "I despair of finding a personal idea in Aron." *Witness to My Life: the Letters of Jean-Paul Sartre to Simone de Beauvoir, 1929–1939* (New York: Charles Scribner's Sons, 1992), p. 430.

19. Raymond Aron, *Marxism and the Existentialists* (New York: Harper and Row, 1969) and *History and the Dialectic of Violence.*

20. de Beauvoir, *La Force de l'Âge,* p. 167.

21. Isaiah Berlin, "Does Political Theory Still Exist?" in Peter Laslett and W. G. Runciman, eds., *Philosophy, Politics and Society,* second series (Oxford: Basil Blackwell, 1969), pp. 9, 17.

22. Sartre, [introduction to] "Les damnés de la terre" in *Situations, V* (Paris: Gallimard, 1964), p. 175.

23. Sartre, *Anti-Semite and Jew* (New York: Schocken Books, 1965), pp. 146, 149, 150–151.

24. Georgi Plekhanov, *The Materialist Conception of History* (New York: International Publishers, 1940), p. 11.

25. Karl Marx to J. Weydemeyer, 5 March 1852.

26. Throughout this section of the chapter, I shall be pilfering from my essay "Red Flags/Black Flags: Marxists against Anarchists," in Roy Macridis and Mark Hulliung, *Contemporary Political Ideologies: Movements and Regimes,* 6th edition (New York: HarperCollins, 1996), ch. 12.

27. Proudhon to Marx, 17 May 1846, in Steward Edwards, ed., *Selected Writings of Pierre-Joseph Proudhon* (New York: Anchor, 1969), pp. 150–151. Bakunin, *Statism and Anarchy* (New York: Cambridge University Press, 1994), pp. 184, 194.

28. Bakunin to Jura anarchists, November 1871. Quoted by James Joll, *The Anarchists* (New York: Grosset & Dunlop, 1966), p. 105.

29. Sam Dolgoff, ed., *Bakunin on Anarchism* (Montréal: Black Rose Books, 1980), p. 352.

30. Marx, "Address of the Central Committee to the Communist League (March 1850) and "Minutes of the Central Committee Meeting of 15 September 1850" in David Fernbach, ed., *Karl Marx: the Revolutions of 1848* (New York: Vintage, 1974), pp. 319–330, 339–344.

31. With the possible complication of Marx's stand on the Paris Commune, which would take too long to discuss.

32. Marx, Engels, Lenin, *Anarchism and Anarcho-Syndicalism* (New York: International Publishers, 1972), pp. 106, 55.

33. *Bakunin on Anarchism*, p. 268.

34. Lenin, *What Is to Be Done?* (New York: International Publishers, 1981). pp. 74, 94 104–105.

35. Rosa Luxemburg, *Leninism or Marxism? [Organizational Questions of Russian Social Democracy]* (Ann Arbor: University of Michigan Press, 1961), pp. 108, 91.

36. Rosa Luxemburg, *The Russian Revolution* (Ann Arbor: University of Michigan Press, 1961), pp. 72, 62, 77.

37. Karl Kautsky, *Terrorism and Communism* (Westport: Hyperion Press, 1973), pp. 206, 214, 231–232.

38. Lenin, *The Proletarian Revolution and the Renegade Kautsky* (Peking: Foreign Languages Press, 1975). Published in 1918 in response to Kautsky's, *The Dictatorship of the Proletariat* (Ann Arbor: University of Michigan Press, 1964), also published in 1918.

39. Kautsky, *Terrorism and Communism,* pp. 92–93, 95, 209.

40. Trotsky, *The Permanent Revolution* (New York: Pathfinder Press, 1976).

41. Stewart Edwards, ed., *Selected Writings of Pierre-Joseph Proudhon,* p. 158. On "spontaneity," pp. 92, 154, 156, 231.

42. Simone de Beauvoir, *La Force des Choses,* vol. 1 (Paris: Gallimard, 1963), p. 15. *La Force de l'Âge,* p. 93.

43. Alain, *Éléments d'une Doctrine Radicale,* 4th ed. (Paris: Gallimard, 1933).

44. Albert Camus, "In Defense of *The Rebel,*" in David A. Sprintzen and Adrian van den Hoven, *Sartre and Camus: A Historic Confrontation* (Amherst, NY: Humanity Books, 2004), p. 215.

45. Sartre, *Notebooks for an Ethics* (Chicago: University of Chicago Press, 1992), pp. 21, 263, 331.

46. de Beauvoir, *La Force de l'Âge,* pp. 50, 89, 292.

47. Ibid., pp. 37, 149.

48. Ibid., pp. 155–156, 171, 413.

49. Ibid., pp. 331, 344.

50. Ibid., pp. 155, 428–429, 572.

51. Sartre, *Situations* (New York: George Braziller, 1965), p. 167.

52. Sartre, *The Transcendence of the Ego* (New York: Farrar, Straus and Giroux, n.d.), p. 105.

53. Sartre, "Paul Nizan," in *Situations* (New York: George Braziller, 1965), pp. 113–173.

54. Sartre, *What Is Literature?* (New York: Harper & Row, 1965), pp. 153–154.

55. *Transcendence of the Ego,* pp. 98-99.

56. *What Is Literature?,* pp. 142, 172, 174, 177n.

57. Ibid., pp. 143–144.

58. Sartre, "The Itinerary of a Thought" in *Between Existentialism and Marxism* (New York: Pantheon, 1974), p. 60.

59. Sartre, "Self-Portrait at Seventy" in *Life/Situations: Essays Written and Spoken* (New York: Pantheon, 1977), pp. 24, 25, 78, 83.

60. Annie Cohen-Solal, *Sartre: A Biography* (New York: Pantheon Books, 1987), p. 388.

61. André Breton, "Second Manifesto of Surrealism" in *Manifestoes of Surrealism* (Ann Arbor: University of Michigan Press, 1972), p. 127.

62. Ibid., p. 129.

63. Sartre, *Critique of Dialectical Reason,* vol. 1 (London: Verso, 1982), p. 349. I have slightly altered the translation. For the original French, *Critique de la raison dialectique* (Paris: Gallimard, 1960), p. 384.

64. Sartre, *The Communists and Peace* (New York: George Braziller, 1968), p. 229.

65. Ibid., pp. 189–190.

66. Sartre, "Réponse à Claude Lefort," reprinted in *Situations, VII* (Paris: Gallimard, 1965), pp. 7–93. An English translation is available in *The Communists and Peace,* pp. 235–296.

67. "A Response to Claude Lefort," pp. 269, 272.

68. *Critique of Dialectical Reason,* vol. 1, pp. 241–249, 680, 688n.

69. Ibid., p. 241.

70. Dolgoff, ed., *Bakunin on Anarchism,* pp. 294, 334.

71. de Beauvoir, *La Force de l'Âge,* p. 172.

72. Sartre, *The Communists and Peace,* pp. 100–101, 113.

73. Ibid., pp. 51n, 128.

74. *The Ghost of Stalin,* p. 33.

75. Ibid., p. 39.

76. Merleau-Ponty, "Sartre et l'ultra-bolchevisme," in *Les Aventures de la Dialectique* (Paris: Gallimard, 1955), ch. 5.

77. *The Communists and Peace,* pp. 90, 275.

78. *Critique of Dialectical Reason,* vol. 1, pp. 519–520, 522–523. *Search for a Method* (New York: Alfred A. Knopf, 1963), p. 43.

79. Sartre, "Faux savants ou faux lièvres" in *Situations, VI* (Paris: Gallimard, 1964), pp. 30, 31, 52, 62, 64, 67. This essay originally appeared in 1950 as the preface to Louis Dalmas, *Le Communisme Yougoslave depuis la Rupture avec Moscou.*

80. Sartre, "France: Masses, Spontaneity, Party," in *Between Existentialism and Marxism* (New York: Pantheon Books, 1975), pp. 119–121.

81. Daniel Cohn-Bendit, *Obsolete [Senile] Communism* (San Francisco: AK Press, 2000), p. 184.

82. *Les Temps Modernes,* vol. 3, pt. 1 (Feb. 1948), p. 1516n. For studies of the *Les Temps Modernes* group, see Michel-Antoine Burnier in his *Choice of Action: The French Existentialists on the Political Front Line* (New York: Random House, 1968); Anna Boschetti, *The Intellectual Enterprise: Sartre and Les Temps Modernes* (Evanston: Northwestern University Press, 1988); Howard Davies, *Sartre and 'Les Temps Modernes'* (Cambridge University Press, 1987).

83. Breton, *Second Manifesto of Surrealism,* p. 125.

84. *What Is Literature?,* pp. 208, 179.

85. Ibid., pp. 142, 179–180, 191, 251.

86. *The Communists and Peace,* pp. 111–114, 116n, 117.

87. The best study is that of Ronald Aronson, *Sartre's Second Critique* (Chicago: University of Chicago Press, 1987).

88. *Critique of Dialectical Reason,* vol. 2, pp. 98, 108.

89. Ibid., pp. 99–100, 196.

90. Ibid., pp. 111, 195.

91. *The Ghost of Stalin,* pp. 119–120.

92. Ibid., p. 78.

93. Ibid., p. 81.

94. Quoted by Annie Cohen-Solal, *Sartre: A Life,* p. 454.

95. Sartre, "Czechoslovakia: the Socialism that Came in From the Cold," in *Between Existentialism and Marxism,* p. 117.

96. Sartre, "Merleau-Ponty," p. 255

97. Annie Cohen-Solal, *Sartre: a Life,* p. 402.

98. de Beauvoir, *La Force de l'Âge,* p. 40.

99. *Critique of Dialectical Reason,* vol. 1, p. 383.

100. Ibid., p. 392.

101. Ibid., pp. 394–395.

102. Ibid., p. 395.

103. In the *New Left Review,* no. 100 (Nov. 1976–Jan. 1977).

104. *Life/Situations,* p. 24.

105. Sartre's position in May 1968 resembles his stand in 1948, when he was a member of the *Rassemblement Démocratique Révolutionnaire,* as recorded in *Entertiens sur la politique* (Paris: Gallimard, 1949).

106. Sartre, *Les Communistes ont Peur de la Révolution* (Paris: Editions John Didier, 1968), p. 10.

107. Ibid., p. 19.

108. Ibid., p. 13.

109. Ibid., p. 22.

110. "Daniel Cohn-Bendit s'entretient avec Jean-Paul Sartre," in *La Révolte Étudiante: les Animateurs Parlent* (Paris: Editions de Seuil, 1968), pp. 86–97. A useful study of May '68 is that of Bernard E. Brown, *Protest in Paris: Anatomy of a Revolt* (Morristown, NJ: General Learning Press, 1974).

111. Sartre, "France: Masses, Spontaneity, Party" in pp. 126–127.

Chapter 6

1. For instance, as Philip Thody noted, Sartre's book on Genet was sometimes taken to be his presentation of an existentialist ethics. *Jean-Paul Sartre: A Literary and Political Study* (London: Hamish Hamilton, 1960), p. 159.

2. Studies of Sartre's late comments on ethics include Thomas C. Anderson, *Sartre's Two Ethics: From Authenticity to Integral Humanity* (La Salle: Open Court, 1993) and Ronald E. Santoni, *Sartre and Violence: Curiously Ambivalent* (University Park: Pennsylvania State University Press, 2003). Also pertinent is William L. McBride, *Sartre's Political Theory* (Bloomington: Indiana University Press, 1991), ch. 6.

3. *Being and Nothingness* (New York: Washington Square Press, 1966), pp. 557–558.

4. Sartre, *L'Existentialisme est un Humanisme* (Paris: Nagel, 1970), p. 28.

5. Ibid., pp. 292, 293.

6. *Anti-Semite and Jew* (New York: Schocken, 1976), pp. 89–90.

7. Maurice Merleau-Ponty, *Humanism and Terror* (Boston: Beacon Press, 1969), pp. xviii, 13, 104.

8. Sartre explicitly abandoned Kantian universalism in his *Notebooks for an Ethics* (Chicago: University of Chicago Press, 1992), p. 426.

9. Excellent on the topic of "will" is Patrick Riley, *Will and Political Legitimacy: A Critical Exposition of Social Contract Theory in Hobbes, Locke, Rousseau, Kant, and Hegel* (Cambridge, MA: Harvard University Press, 1982).

10. Sartre, "The Theory of the State in Modern French Thought" in Michel Contat and Michel Rybalka, eds., *The Writings of Jean-Paul Sartre,* vol. 2 (Evanston: Northwestern University Press, 1974), p. 22.

11. Ibid., p. 36.

12. Annie Cohen-Solal, *Sartre: A Life* (New York: Pantheon Books, 1987), pp. 166, 169–170, 181. "Conversations with Jean-Paul Sartre" in Simone de Beauvoir, *Adieux* (New York: Pantheon Books, 1984), p. 392.

13. *The War Diaries of Jean-Paul Sartre: November 1939/March 1940* (New York: Pantheon Books, 1984), p. 294. Steward Edwards, ed., *Selected Writings of Pierre-Joseph Proudhon* (New York: Anchor, 1969), p. 263.

14. Proudhon, *General Idea of the Revolution in the Nineteenth Century* (London: Pluto Press, 1989), pp. 112–115, 171, 192, 200, 205, 244–246, 268, 273, 288, 292, 295. *Selected Writings of Pierre-Joseph Proudhon,* pp. 116–117.

15. *Being and Nothingness,* p. 749. Sartre did not seem to understand that Proudhon's position in *What Is Property?* was that land should never become private.

16. *Notebooks for an Ethics,* p. 414.

17. Ibid., pp. 264, 271.

18. Ibid., pp. 142, 143, 145, 177.

19. *La Nausée* (Paris: Gallimard, 1938) Folio (1987), pp. 187, 125.

20. Sartre, "L'enfance d'un chef," in *Le Mur* (Paris: Gallimard, 1939) Livre de Poche (1967), pp. 247–248.

21. *Sartre on Cuba* (New York: Ballantine Books, 1961), pp. 36, 95, 133, 148.

22. Sartre, "Portrait du colonisé" and "Le colonialisme est un système" in *Situations, V* (Paris: Gallimard, 1964), pp. 44, 52–55.

23. *Critique of Dialectical Reason,* vol. 1 (London: Verso, 1982), pp. 420, 441.

24. E.g., Mark Poster, *Existential Marxism in Postwar France: From Sartre to Althusser* (Princeton, NJ: Princeton University Press, 1975), p. 301. William L. McBride, *Sartre's Political Theory,* pp. 143, 153.

25. *Critique of Dialectical Reason,* vol. 1, p. 799.

26. Ibid., p. 420.

27. Raymond Aron, *History and the Dialectic of Violence* (New York: Harper Torchbooks, 1976), pp. 66–67.

28. Wilfrid Desan, *The Marxism of Jean-Paul Sartre* (Garden City, NY: Doubleday & Company, 1965), ch. 10.

29. E.g., Ronald Aronson, *Sartre's Second Critique* (Chicago: University of Chicago Press, 1987), p. 72.

30. *Sartre on Cuba,* pp. 38, 95, 97, 100, 103, 107, 149.

31. *Critique of Dialectical Reason,* vol. 1, pp. 419, 467. Aron, *History and the Dialectic of Violence,* pp. 109–110.

32. *Critique of Dialectical Reason,* vol. 1, p. 437.

33. *The Communists and Peace* (New York: George Braziller, 1968), p. 228.

34. "Le Constitution du mépris" in *Situations, V* (Paris: Gallimard, 1964), p. 112.

35. *Critique of Dialectical Reason,* vol. 1, p. 485.

36. *Critique of Dialectical Reason,* vol. 2 (London: Verso, 1991), p. 199.

37. *Critique of Dialectical Reason,* vol. 1, p. 628.

38. Ibid., pp. 630, 636–637.

39. Ibid., pp. 610, 636, 637, 661.

40. Quoted by Michel-Antoine Burnier, *Choice of Action: The French Existentialists on the Political Front Line* (New York: Random House, 1968), p. 86.

41. *Critique of Dialectical Reason,* vol. 1, p. 661.

42. Ibid., pp. 610, 612.

43. Quoted by Annie Cohen-Solal, *Sartre: A Biography,* p. 462.

44. Sartre, "Justice and the State," in *Life/Situations* (New York: Pantheon Books, 1977), p. 179.

45. Sartre, *The Family Idiot,* vol. I (Chicago: University of Chicago Press, 1981), p. 341; vol. IV, pp. 26, 106; vol. V, pp. 446, 467.

Index

About the Author

Mark Hulliung is the Richard Koret Professor of the History of Ideas at Brandeis University. He has published widely on topics concerning intellectual, cultural, and political history, both European and American, including the interactions between America and Europe. He is a historian and a political theorist, and his work is interdisciplinary in nature, cutting especially across history, political science, and literary studies.

Printed in the United States
by Baker & Taylor Publisher Services